# TIERED LEARNING STATIONS in Minutes!

## Increasing Achievement, High-Level Thinking, and the Joy of Learning

**Bertie Kingore**
AUTHOR

**Jeffery Kingore**
GRAPHIC DESIGN

Current Publications by
**Bertie Kingore, Ph.D.**

VISIT DR. KINGORE ONLINE!
**www.bertiekingore.com**

*Alphabetters: Thinking Adventures with the Alphabet* (Task cards)
*Assessment: Timesaving Procedures for Busy Teachers*, 4th ed.
*Assessment Interactive CD-ROM*
*Centers CD-ROM Vol. 1: Grades K-8*
*Centers CD-ROM Vol. 2: Literacy Stations, Grades K-4*
*Developing Portfolios for Authentic Assessment, PreK-3: Guiding Potential in Young Learners*
*Differentiation: Simplified, Realistic, and Effective*
*DIfferentiation Interactive CD-ROM*
*Engaging Creative Thinking: Activities to Integrate Creative Problem Solving*
*Integrating Thinking: Strategies that Work!* 2nd ed.
*Just What I Need! Learning Experiences to Use on Multiple Days in Multiple Ways*
*Kingore Observation Inventory (KOI)*, 3rd ed.
*Literature Celebrations: Catalysts for High-Level Book Responses*, 2nd ed.
*Reading Strategies for Advanced Primary Readers*
*Reading Strategies for Advanced Primary Readers: Professional Development Guide*
*Reaching All Learners: Making Differentiation Work!*
*Recognizing Gifted Potential: Planned Experiences with the KOI*
*Recognizing Gifted Potential: Professional Development Presentation*
*Rigor and Engagement for Growing Minds: Strategies that Enable High-Ability Learners to Flourish in All Classrooms*
*Rigor and Engagement for Growing Minds: Facilitator's Guide for a Book Study*
*Rigor and Engagement for Growing Minds: Professional Development Presentation*
*We Care: A Curriculum for Preschool Through Kindergarten*, 2nd ed.

FOR INFORMATION OR ORDERS CONTACT:
**PA PUBLISHING**
PO Box 28056
Austin, Texas 78755-8056
Phone/fax: 866-335-1460

VISIT US ONLINE!
**www.kingore.com**

## *Tiered Learning Stations in Minutes!*
### *Increasing Achievement, High-Level Thinking, and the Joy of Learning*

Copyright © 2011 Bertie Kingore

Published by **PROFESSIONAL ASSOCIATES PUBLISHING**

Printed in the United States of America
ISBN: 978-0-9787042-7-8

# Tiered Learning Stations in Minutes
*Increase Achievement, High-Level Thinking, and the Joy of Learning*
*Grades K-8*

# Contents

# *1*
# *Introduction*

## LEARNING STATIONS: RESEARCH AND BEST PRACTICES

> Learning stations are classroom work sites where students complete
> significant learning objectives and flexible group interactions
> away from their usual table or desk.
>
> Tiered stations incorporate learning experiences that
> promote continuous learning for all students
> at appropriate but different levels of complexity.
> All students learn the same concepts and skills
> at the varied levels of complexity that respond to their readiness.

While students typically love centers, observing adults might wonder how much real learning occurs, and teachers can feel overwhelmed by the intensive preparation required to implement many centers. Consequently, *Tiered Learning Stations in Minutes* shares station-based learning strategies and experiences that emphasize student achievement and high-level thinking rather than the interior decorating skills of the teacher. Appealing visual stimuli and simple decorations are incorporated to add interest, but the crucial objective is for students to explore, discover, practice, apply, master, or extend concepts and skills related to the curriculum.

A learning station is a physical area of the classroom organized with materials and learning experiences that enable students to respond to specific instructional objectives through individual work and small group experiences. Stations enable children to work in a variety of flexible groups rather than a stagnated placement in the same group. Membership in learning station groups should change frequently. At different times, groupings in learning stations are based upon mixed-readiness levels, similar-readiness levels, or interests to minimize any stigma being attached to group membership. Small groups allow students working together at a station to intervene with appropriate support for struggling peers but can also provide peer support appropriate for students whose learning capacities extend to grade level and beyond (Winebrenner & Brulles, 2008).

Kingore, B. (2011). *Tiered Learning Stations in Minutes*. Austin, TX: PA Publishing.

**Increase achievement through small group interactions.**

Compared to whole class instruction, higher achievement gains occur when students work in groups of two to four (NRP, 2000). The small group setting invites peer collaborations, interactions, and quiet, task-oriented conversations among learners. These interactions elicit mental engagement and provide a social experience that typically increases students' enjoyment of learning. Students' joy in learning is significant since long-term memory is activated when an emotional response is integrated into a learning experience (Sylwester, 2003; Willis, 2007b).

**Increase achievement through tiered learning tasks.**

All students can learn, but not all are at the same point along their learning pathway. Research documents that while the brain's retention increases by connecting the unknown to the known, what specific information is known or unknown differs because of students' diverse background experiences (Caine, Caine, Klimek, & McClintic, 2004; Payne, 2003; Slocumb, 2008; Sousa, 2006). To promote continuous learning for all students and respond to learners' diverse profiles and interests, effective stations include multiple content-rich learning tasks at a wide range of challenge. The tiered tasks are layered on a learning continuum that frequently extends from below-through-beyond grade level to insure success and continued learning. These learning tasks provide a means for students to increase achievement and autonomy as students learn essential concepts and skills. To promote higher-level thinking, learning stations incorporate open-ended inquiry and student-generated responses.

**Contribute to a needs-satisfying classroom.**

Students have five basic needs: belonging/connecting, power/competence, freedom, fun, and survival/safety (Sullo, 2009). Stations support a needs-satisfying classroom as students work with peers, experience the freedom of choice, and engage in enjoyable tasks that are structured for their success.

**Address and respect students' diversity.**

Tiered learning stations respond to today's diverse student memberships by promoting a range of complexity in students' learning responses. Today's standards demand more than memorization of facts and skills. The ideal is for all students to experience continuous learning success that substantiates to them that their effort results in achievement (Dweck, 2007; Sullo, 2009). To ensure continuous learning growth, tiered tasks must challenge students to work slightly above their comfort level rather than respond at or below their current achievement level (Berk & Winsler, 1995; Willis, 2007a). The tasks must be challenging but attainable. Finding an optimal match between child and challenge, also known as the *zone of*

*proximal development,* is crucial (Vygotsky,1962). Since this zone varies for different children, students must experience instructional applications that accommodate different levels of complexity.

### Activate high-level thinking.

Tiered tasks are most effective when they elicit all students' high-level thinking, organization, and decision-making. These valued life skills are promoted at learning stations when students are actively engaged in problem-solving tasks at appropriate readiness levels. Effective learning tasks require high-level thinking for all students because knowledge and skills are necessary but not sufficient elements of understanding for long-term retention and achievement (Shepard, 1997; Wiggins & McTighe, 2005; Willis, 2006). Plan high-appeal learning tasks that require students to generate responses as they interact. Hands-on activities require minds-on applications and enhance learning within a rigorous, relevant curriculum (Wolfe, 2001).

### Integrate assessment and station learning experiences.

Students' self-assessment fosters achievement gains as it requires students to increase their involvement and ownership in evaluation procedures (Sullo, 2009). Research supports that students who consistently evaluate their own achievement become better achievers through the process (Marzano, 2006; Stiggins, 2007). As they complete station tasks, integrate self-assessment by requiring students to write reflections of what they have learned and to self-evaluate the quality of their process and product. Self-evaluation is a productive strategy that results in personal motivation and higher achievement for many students.

### Reinforce social and emotional connections.

Some educators debate whether centers are social or learning-based experiences. Perhaps, there should be no debate as both are readily incorporated. School is a place where students learn together. When more than one student is at a learning station, socialization is invited in the context of learning discussions rather than only as social exchanges. Research supports the value of students collectively analyzing content and communicating using the specific terminology related to a field of study. There is a direct relationship between the development of academic vocabulary and achievement gains in all content areas (ASCD, 2006; Gifford & Gore, 2008; Marzano, 2004; National Reading Panel, 2000; Sousa, 2006). Research also documents that students' learning improves in the presence of positive relationships (Sullo, 2009).

### Support English Language Learners.

Learning stations are advantageous for English Language Learners and dual language classrooms. The small-group setting provides a relatively risk-free environment that invites students to

Kingore, B. (2011). *Tiered Learning Stations in Minutes*. Austin, TX: PA Publishing.

experiment with languages and build academic vocabulary as they discuss content and skills (*Education Week*, 2009). Placing bilingual learners and students with limited English skills together at learning stations provides needed support for successful interactions.

### Respond to students' learning profiles.

The stations cater to individual learning styles and talents by including activities structured around different learning modalities. Teachers incorporate multiple learning pathways because the more ways information is introduced to the brain, the more dendritic pathways of access are created to enhance memory (Willis, 2006). A well-developed learning station provides students with valuable content, challenging tiered tasks, choice, and ongoing opportunities for support, interaction, and feedback. Teachers include appropriate materials at stations that enable students to explore and produce as they extend their autonomy. These learning opportunities are popular with most students because stations incorporate diverse ways to learn and allow students to move to different locations in the classroom.

### Invite learning through academic games.

The small-group interactions characteristic of learning stations are a perfect venue for students to engage in academic games that apply and reinforce concepts and skills. Research studies confirm that using academic games in the classroom increases achievement gains and builds academic vocabulary (ASCD, 2006; Marzano, 2010). Students experience the greatest enjoyment when the game process is fun competition rather than a high-stakes winner-loser designation. Increase the educational value of games by requiring students to debrief the process at the conclusion of a game.

### Connect the curriculum to learning station topics and themes.

Learning stations, such as writing, math, research, art, and reading-listening stations, can remain year-round or they can be topical and change periodically. Incorporate combinations of both by adding topical items or tasks to year-round stations. Stations may relate to the overarching conceptual theme of the class, reflect specific content topics, or relate to one concept or skill by providing varied experiences in the parts of that whole.

### Enable cost-effective applications with equipment.

With tight budgets, learning stations are a cost-effective solution as students can collaboratively use a minimum of equipment. For example, a few microscopes can be incorporated into a standing science station so all students use them at different times and are more actively involved; three class computers can become a station for word processing and technology applications; art activities are often less complicated, less messy, and more manageable when only a few children complete them at one time.

---

Kingore, B. (2011). *Tiered Learning Stations in Minutes*. Austin, TX: PA Publishing.

## *KEY POINTS THAT ENHANCE ACHIEVEMENT GAINS*

Providing stations and having students *do activities* is not sufficient to affect long-term learning. To elicit the greatest gains and increase the achievement of students through tiered learning stations, implement the following key points.

- **Discuss targeted learning objectives.**
Learning stations have little effect on achievement if they are void of academic content. Post objectives and skills at each station, and make students responsible for explaining how they addressed the objectives and applied the skills (CCSO & NGA, 2010). Emphasize the academic language of the topic, and ask students to incorporate specific content terminology as they interact at a station or complete written tasks. For example, challenge students to explain the experiment in the words a scientist would use. Additionally, provide an audience for students' applications by inviting any adult visiting the classroom to ask students to explain how they incorporated the objective and targeted skills in their work at the station.

- **Debrief the content and process.**
Debriefing helps students process and retain information. When stations conclude, debrief to expedite problem-solving and refine the learning process as students review the content. Involve the class in a brief oral discussion of their learning experiences  For example, the teacher or a student might stimulate process analysis by asking students to:
  - Share a strategy they used successfully,
  - Identify the hardest part,
  - Share what they noticed about the task,
  - Explain an obstacle and how they overcame it, or
  - Explain what they did well.

- **Elicit student feedback and self-assessment.**
Instruct students to maintain a written log in which they record what they learned during a station experience or which parts of the task were difficult or easy and why. In these station logs, students also record their self-assessments of their process and product according to the provided rubrics. The Tool Box CD included with this book provides examples of templates for a log of reflections to guide students' awareness of how their effort results in achievement and in what ways they are changing as learners.

- **Adjust learning tasks.**
Review student logs to guide the level of learning opportunities provided at learning stations by revising the pace or adjusting the thinking levels, complexity, and depth according to students' feedback. At times, the feedback may signal a need for intervention, reteaching, or additional resources.

Kingore, B. (2011). *Tiered Learning Stations in Minutes*. Austin, TX: PA Publishing.

- **Revise understandings.**

Students benefit from opportunities to revisit their notes and revise their understanding of the content (Marzano, 2010). Periodically, invite students to skim their station log notes, class notes, or lab reports and make whatever changes they can to reflect their current understanding. Rather than it being a negative, emphasize that students are demonstrating learning growth when they correct misconceptions or embellish prior information.

- **Incorporate student-developed portfolios.**

The products students produce at learning stations are authentic indicators of their interests, capabilities, and mastery or extension of required skills and concepts. Inasmuch as learning station experiences are based upon significant concepts and skills, the resulting products evolve into a student portfolio that more authentically documents achievement than traditional assessment procedures alone (Kingore 2008; Kingore 2007). At the conclusion of a topic, instruct students to select one learning station product to include in their portfolios. This understandable evidence is a valued source of assessment information for students, teachers, and parents (Stiggins, 2007). Over time, student portfolios document continued progress and learning dispositions.

 *Caution!* To be appropriate for advanced students, learning stations must include complex, tiered activities and beyond-grade-level resources. Provide an ample variety of nonfiction materials that enable these students to extend their learning and satisfy their voracious appetites for specific information. Provide some opportunities for advanced learners to work together at the same learning station to promote greater complexity and depth.

## CONCLUSION

Learning stations are not new to teachers, but tiered stations that teachers prepare in minutes to enable students to practice and extend learning standards may be unique and desperately needed. Essential features of this book include tiered learning experiences that integrate significant learning objectives to increase achievement, techniques that require less intensive preparation, and management systems that increase students' organization and productivity. Instead of spending the many hours typically required to prepare and decorate stations, teachers benefit from learning stations that minimize preparation while accelerating students' minds into a high gear for learning. As examples, this book includes plans for twenty tiered learning stations-in-minutes plus twelve station ideas especially for young learners. These plans enable teachers to develop tiered, content-rich learning stations that increase achievement while saving time, energy, and expense. Figure 1.1 lists the educational values of learning stations and summarizes the key points of station-based learning.

Kingore, B. (2011). *Tiered Learning Stations in Minutes*. Austin, TX: PA Publishing.

## • Figure 1.1 •
# THE VALUE OF LEARNING STATIONS
*Learning stations promote invaluable learning moments and*
*increase achievement in a differentiated learning environment.*

✓ The provided learning station tasks integrate a majority of district or state standards and learning objectives so students actively explore, discover, practice, apply, master, or extend the concepts and skills related to the curriculum.

✓ These learning experiences promote students' high-level thinking, responsibility, autonomy, organization, and decision-making skills as students are actively engaged in problem-solving tasks.

✓ Students increase their ability to work independently and in a variety of flexible groups to learn from and support each other.

✓ Stations should include learning experiences that incorporate multiple modalities and provide opportunities for continuous learning through students' best ways to learn.

✓ Learning stations allow students to learn at locations other than their usual desks or table areas. The change from sitting at a desk to standing at a station or working on the floor revitalizes some children's engagement in learning.

✓ Learning stations and small group interactions increase the social and emotional connections to learning that brain research deems vital to long-term learning.

✓ Multiple languages can be practiced and applied as bilingual students provide peer support to English Language Learners.

✓ Introspective students may feel more comfortable expressing ideas within a small group than before the entire class.

✓ Learning stations incorporate students' interests by using tasks based upon interest surveys. For example, Research in Action becomes a station that includes nonfiction resources related to students' expressed interests.

✓ Learning station tasks enable choice and increase student ownership as students select among the several learning experiences provided at a station.

✓ Learning stations differentiate through tiered learning tasks that incorporate the same concepts and skills at varying levels of complexity in response to learners' readiness.

✓ Learning stations are cost-effective as students collaboratively use a minimum of equipment.

Kingore, B. (2011). *Tiered Learning Stations in Minutes*. Austin, TX: PA Publishing.

*Idea!* Share a list of the value of learning stations with parents and administrators so they understand that these stations provide significant, standards-based learning opportunities that lead to higher achievement.

## QUALITY LEARNING OPPORTUNITIES

> The quality of the learning opportunity
> determines the level of students' responses.
> If we fail to provide learning experiences
> that promote high-level thinking and challenge,
> we will have to be content with basic student responses
> instead of excellence.

### To Use or Not to Use Folder Games and Matching Tasks: A Personal Reflection

During my third year of teaching, I reached a startling conclusion—I was spending three hours to create a learning task for a center that students spent three minutes completing the next day. I realized that most center tasks based upon folder games or matching tasks promoted simple correct answers instead of high-level thinking and problem-solving skills. Equally damaging, these simple one-answer tasks reinforced a short attention span. I certainly did not intend for students' attention spans to be reduced to three minutes.

I began challenging myself to think differently. What kinds of experiences would engage students in meaningful learning opportunities and lead to higher achievement?

### The Challenge

> Make learning in small groups and at learning stations
> as rich and productive as if it were teacher-directed.

### To Successfully Respond to this Challenge:

• Ponder which essential learning standards are best incorporated into learning station experiences and determine how to implement engaging activities that build those concepts and skills rather than continue with activities that largely serve to keep children busy (CCSO & NGA, 2010).

Kingore, B. (2011). *Tiered Learning Stations in Minutes.* Austin, TX: PA Publishing.

- Provide all students with respectful learning experiences that are developmentally appropriate and more open-ended to encourage student success at different levels with high-level thinking and multiple correct responses.

- Elicit more high-level thinking and student-generated products instead of emphasizing adult decorations and students' neat work.

- Implement some learning experiences that engage students in longer think-time yet minimize writing as many children's hands wear out before their heads. More writing does not inherently mean greater productivity.

## The Reward for this Effort

- Students who are mentally engaged in learning are more motivated to achieve at higher levels and feel more ownership in *their* centers. Fewer behavior problems arise when children are meaningfully involved.

- Students take pride in posting their work so other students and visiting adults can reflect and respond to it. (This process can result in less to grade.)

- Teachers are able to develop learning stations in minutes instead of dedicating an entire summer or most weekends to producing folder games and making decorations to change their centers. Tiered stations-in-minutes incorporate tasks that require high-level thinking and problem solving at appropriate degrees of challenge. Hence, these stations result in extended students' engagement so that learning tasks need to change less frequently.

Kingore, B. (2011). *Tiered Learning Stations in Minutes.* Austin, TX: PA Publishing.

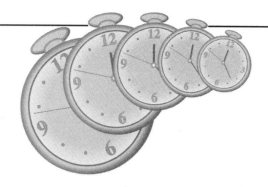

# APPLICATION TIME: REFLECT AND SELECT

## 3-2-1

**3 key ideas I need to remember**

3 _____

_____

_____

_____

_____

_____

**2 practices I will implement**

2 _____

_____

_____

_____

**1 thing I want to read more about**

1 _____

_____

Kingore, B. (2011). *Tiered Learning Stations in Minutes*. Austin, TX: PA Publishing.

# *Initiating Station-Based Learning*

## WAYS TO MAKE ROOM FOR LEARNING STATIONS

**A TEACHER LAMENTS:**
*"I don't have enough*
*room*
*for learning stations!"*

Avoid thinking of learning stations as areas with permanent furniture that require a great deal of classroom space, such as a house keeping center in a prekindergarten classroom. When regular classrooms lack extra space, creatively use corners and crannies to make room for stations.

### 1. Standing Stations

Use counter tops, the tops of book shelves, and extended window sill areas as standing stations. Post a sign with the name of the station, place activities along the area, and students stand to complete learning tasks.

### 2. Corner

Add pillows and clipboards to a corner area to make a small station. An area rug adds to the visual interest of this area. A corner station is a great choice for games and manipulatives that work well on the floor.

### 3. Bulletin Board

A bulletin board can become an interactive learning station that invites students to apply the high-level thinking skills of similarities and differences. Research documents that the strategy of analyzing the similarities and differences of topics and concepts results in the greatest increase in achievement (Marzano, 2004). A bulletin board learning station can require the categorization and comparative thinking skills that lead to understanding similarities and differences. Students use push pins or self-sticking clips to appropriately categorize pictures and small items on a bulletin board divided with yarn into two or more areas.

### 4. Multi-purpose Furniture

In a regular classroom, space can be obtained by abolishing the idea of ownership: one desk for each child. Cluster the students' tables or desks to create learning stations. The desks or tables take on a multi-purpose use instead of the *one-student, one-desk, one-location* organization of the past. In a learning station environment, a desk is used by one student completing independent work, then that desk is clustered with others to become part of a research lab, and later becomes part of a cooperative learning group task.

### 5. Peg Board or Felt Board

Cover the back of a piece of furniture with a piece of peg board or felt to gain a potential learning station. Book shelves work particularly well for this conversion. Place the converted furniture perpendicular to the wall so both sides become useable as two different stations. (Felt can also be clipped with binder clips to the bottom rail of the dry erase board.)

### 6. Metal Filing Cabinet

Use the sides of a filing cabinet for magnetic manipulatives. Magnetic letters and numerals enable students to apply skills including alphabetizing, spelling, word building, math word problems, and sets. A magnetic hook or clip is a useful place to hang a bag containing the manipulatives.

### 7. Learning Station on a Shelf

Plastic bins, unused pizza boxes, shoe boxes, and shirt boxes create stations on a shelf. Students select a station box and move to an open floor or desk area to work. When finished, they return the station box to the shelf.

*Idea!* Label both the container and the designated place on the shelf with the task's name so boxes are easily returned to their appropriate places.

*Caution!* With young children and students who have physical limitations, shirt boxes do not work as well for a station as they are more flimsy and prone to spilling when being carried.

Kingore, B. (2011). *Tiered Learning Stations in Minutes*. Austin, TX: PA Publishing.

## 8. Expandable Folder Station

Expandable folders are similar to stations on a shelf in that they require a minimum storage area. They are most effective as stations that only require paper and small items, such as stations based upon task cards. Clearly label and store the folders for these stations in a filing drawer or crate for students to access, use, and return.

## 9. Privacy Place

Some younger children like to crawl inside spaces and occasionally need the opportunity to choose time alone to complete work effectively. Consider providing a place that allows privacy for an individual child. This can be accomplished through a big cardboard box with a door and window cut out so one child might go inside the box. As an alternative, extend a table cloth or sheet well over the edges of a table so a child can sit or lay underneath to complete learning tasks.

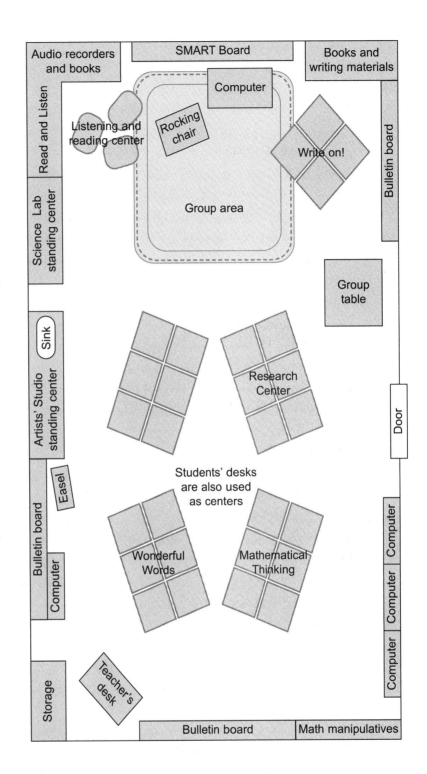

Kingore, B. (2011). *Tiered Learning Stations in Minutes*. Austin, TX: PA Publishing.

## LOCATION OF LEARNING STATIONS

Consider the following factors when determining the location of learning stations.

- **Location and availability of equipment**

  The equipment students need at a specific station may dictate its location, such as being near a computer, sink, electrical outlet, bulletin board, or interactive white board.

- **Noise potential and the activity level required at a station**

  Typically, place stations with greater potential for noise or physical activity further away from any area where an adult or student conducts a direct lesson with a small group.

- **Architectural features of the classroom**

  Features in the room such as windows, doors, and storage areas can be limitations when locating stations, or they can be planned into the application of the station. For example, a window sill becomes a place to post a station sign and related photographs, task cards, or information. Windows are advantageous locations for science discovery stations to view weather and seasonal changes as well as allow light for seed growth and prism experiments.

- **Traffic patterns within the room**

  Avoid placing station activities in the traffic areas of the classroom or in areas that might result in a safety issue, such as blocking the door.

- **Availability of space in different areas of the room**

  Some stations, such as geometric activities with floor blocks, require a larger area.

- **The students' views**

  Locate stations so they cause the least distraction to students working independently at their desks or with a teacher in an instructional group. If students face the front of the room, for example, stations along the sides and back of the room would be less of a distraction and encourage more productivity.

- **The teacher's view**

  Avoid placing stations where the view of the whole classroom is obstructed. It is advantageous to be able to quickly scan the classroom while working with others.

## GUIDELINES FOR INSTRUCTIONALLY VIBRANT STATIONS

Instructionally vibrant learning stations increase student achievement. Learning stations that fail to focus on essential academic content and students' learning profiles have little effect on achievement and squander valuable learning time. Consequently, each station must integrate significant content with targeted learning standards and be designed to ensure that all students succeed at their optimum learning levels. To nurture students' success, include joyful learning experiences for students and incorporate techniques that promote their responsibility for record keeping and self management. To ensure continuous learning for all students, provide a range of tiered tasks that are appropriate to the diverse readiness levels of students. The following guidelines promote instructionally vibrant stations.

## Focus on essential learning outcomes

Emphasize objectives that are integral to the curriculum. Ensure that students are not just *doing activities*.

> *Learning is not maximized when stations are simply convenient places to send students to keep them busy.*

## Document concepts and skills

Document that standards are emphasized in the content of each station by posting a laminated list of the concepts and skills that can be incorporated. Post an applicable list of learning standards at students' eye-level in each different station, and use a wipe-off pen to check the skills incorporated into the content of the current learning experiences. As the learning tasks evolve, change the checked standards. In this way, a learning standards poster communicates to the students which skills and concepts they are expected to understand and apply as they work at the station. It also clearly signals visiting adults that specific learning objectives are in progress during learning station sessions. The Tool Box CD includes examples to prompt applications of learning standards posters.

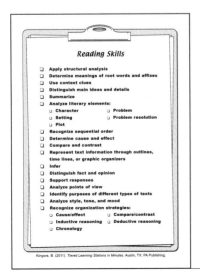

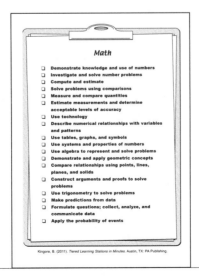

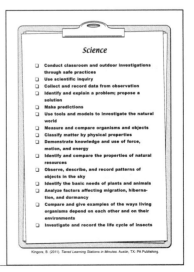

Kingore, B. (2011). *Tiered Learning Stations in Minutes*. Austin, TX: PA Publishing.

*Idea!* Share copies of the learning standards posters with administrators. Explain the process of using the posters to communicate learning standards to students and parents so administrators understand how teachers embed concepts and skills into specific learning tasks at stations.

- **Promote high-level thinking.**

   All students benefit from multiple learning opportunities to use higher-level thinking skills when working with content, process, and products.

## Integrate assessment and station experiences

- **Provide a learning behavior rubric.**

   Transform classroom management rules into a rubric that clearly defines positive learning behaviors for students working without direct teacher instruction. Post a rubric of effective learning behaviors on the wall and/or provide a copy to include in students' station logs. When students concretely see the preferred behaviors and levels of quality, they are more likely to work to achieve a higher level. Most students can hit a target that we make clear to them. Students should use the learning behavior rubric daily to evaluate their goals and work behaviors. The Tool Box CD contains different examples of learning behavior rubrics from simple to more expanded and complex levels.

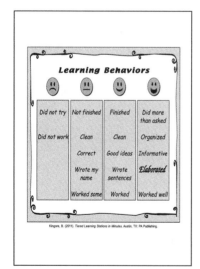
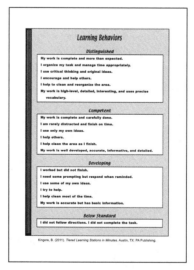

*Idea!* Share a copy of the learning behavior rubric with parents so they can support their child's learning behaviors and efforts to learn.

- **Provide a product rubric.**

   Require students to self-evaluate the products they produce. Provide product rubrics that define quality work for students before they begin learning tasks. Students review a copy of the rubric and check personal goals for what they intend to accomplish as they work on the product. When they complete the learning experience, they use a second color to self-evaluate their level of success on the same copy of the rubric to emphasize that the grade they earn relates to their effort.

- **Ensure that learning tasks are interesting and important.**
  Include a range of interactive learning tasks that appeal to the interests, diverse learning profiles, and readiness levels of the students. Students should perceive that the work is important and worth doing well.

- **Provide clear directions.**
  Students need clear directions to understand how to proceed at stations. It may be advisable to develop step-by-step procedures and checklists that students use to monitor their progress.

- **Promote students' organization.**
  Encourage students' organization skills by including places for completed work and needed supplies, such as a cork board, boxes, in and out bins, metal rings, and folders.

- **Develop class routines.**
  Establish routines for participating at learning stations so students understand expected behaviors such as where to go, what to do, and how long to stay.

- **Motivate excellence by providing audiences for learning products.**
  Require students to display much of the work they complete at stations. Displaying work motivates quality responses and provides an audience for students' accomplishments. It enables students to share their responses and products with others rather than only produce more papers for the teacher to grade. The displayed work also generates topic-related discussion among students.

*Idea!* A small cork board at a station works well as a display center. When cork boards are not feasible, provide a putty-like adhesive in each center to enable students to adhere their papers to the wall without damaging surfaces.

*Caution!* Insure that the tiered learning experiences are planned to enable all students to successfully complete work if they think and make an appropriate effort. A display would have a negative effect if some students were required to post work they could not do well.

Kingore, B. (2011). *Tiered Learning Stations in Minutes.* Austin, TX: PA Publishing.

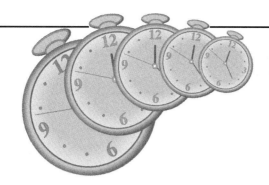

## APPLICATION TIME: REFLECT AND SELECT

# First Things First

**My Priorities and Sequence for Implementation:**

✓ **First**

✓ **Next**

✓ **Details**

# • 3 •
# *Understanding Tiered Instruction*

Tiered instruction is a strategy that aligns the complexity of learning tasks to the readiness levels of students. The teacher preassesses to determine what students know and then prescribes content, processes, and products at students' different readiness levels. Instead of all students completing the same learning task in the same way, variations of learning tasks adapt to the skill level and learning style of students to enable all students to experience continuous learning of essential academic content. To promote continuous learning for all students at each tiered learning station:

✓ Provide varied levels of experiences to align to each student's readiness and best way to learn,

✓ Incorporate different support systems and structures to expedite learning, and

✓ Allow students to focus on the same concepts and skills at different levels of complexity.

Tiered stations are an effective mixed-readiness grouping application inasmuch as the tiered learning experiences make it realistic for different students demonstrating a range of readiness levels to learn at the same station. Tiering does not make the work easier; it provides appropriate levels of challenge so students thrive (Wormeli, 2006). It customizes how students learn concepts and skills; it does not compromise what is learned.

The complexity of tiered tasks is relative to the content at the learning station and students' learning profiles. In a classroom with struggling students, the lowest tier reflects the needs of struggling students. In classes in which all students are at or above grade level, the lowest tier reflects grade-level or beyond grade-level readiness. Inasmuch as students' assessed readiness is not static and content complexity changes with topics, the number of tiers and the degree of complexity within a tier must vary to respond to the content and the students.

## ELEMENTS OF TIERED INSTRUCTION

There are specific elements that influence the complexity of tiered learning tasks, and those elements are different if the teacher conducts direct instruction or if students work without direct teacher instruction. Figure 3.1 presents the six elements of tiered instruction that are most applicable to learning stations where students work without direct teacher instruction. These elements are further explained through applications that progress from simple to more complex and are listed under each element.

Kingore, B. (2011). *Tiered Learning Stations in Minutes.* Austin, TX: PA Publishing.

• **Figure 3.1** •

# *Tiered Elements: A Continuum of Complexity**

*Adapted from: Kingore, B. (2007). *Reaching all learners: Making differentiation work.*
Austin, TX: PA Publishing.

**Background knowledge and skills**
➡ The task requires entry-level skills. It provides opportunities to develop background toward grade-level expectations.
　➡ Basic information and understanding is required.
　　➡ Grade-level information and understanding is necessary.
　　　➡ Beyond grade-level expertise is required.

**Support system**
➡ An instructional aide or other adult facilitates instruction.
　➡ A recording of the text or task directions is available to students needing clarification.
　　➡ Peers work in pairs to assist each other throughout the task.
　　　➡ A peer task assistant problem solves with students when needed.
　　　　➡ Peers at the station help each other as needed.
　　　　　➡ Individuals are autonomous and work independently.

**Structure or complexity of the process**
➡ Students use a well-known and practiced process. They know what to do.
　➡ The process is less practiced but requires only a few simple steps.
　　➡ The task is less familiar but the parameters of the task are detailed and prescribed.
　　　➡ The parameters are open-ended to encourage student adaptations, as with open-ended graphic organizers.
　　　➡ The process is a new experience and requires multiple steps.
　　　　➡ The process requires sophisticated research skills and independent work behaviors.

Kingore, B. (2011). *Tiered Learning Stations in Minutes.* Austin, TX: PA Publishing.

**Concrete or abstract thinking**

➥ Students require concrete, hands-on experiences and manipulatives.

➥ Students use application and analysis requiring concrete thinking.

➥ Students' complex thinking requires synthesis and evaluation.

➥ Students use deductive and inductive reasoning.

➥ Students use abstract thinking and interpretation.

➥ Students use metaphorical thinking and symbolism.

**Resources**

➥ Students use a provided resource that requires below grade-level readability.

➥ Students are provided with grade-level resources that have topic sentences and key passages highlighted.

➥ Students use the provided grade-level resources.

➥ Students must research to access resources.

➥ Students use resources that require above grade-level readability..

➥ Students use resources that are concept dense and incorporate complex-level vocabulary.

➥ Students research resources requiring sophisticated applications of technology and academic vocabulary.

**Complexity of product**

➥ The product requires basic information and fill-in-the-blank responses.

➥ The product is one that is well-known and frequently completed.

➥ The product integrates grade-level skills and concepts.

➥ The product requires students to generate original responses.

➥ Students produce original adaptations of a familiar product, such as a more complex graphic organizer, and then complete that product using assigned content.

➥ The product is original, complex, and integrates advanced vocabulary, skills, and concepts.

Kingore, B. (2011). *Tiered Learning Stations in Minutes*. Austin, TX: PA Publishing.

## *EXAMPLES THAT INCORPORATE TIERED ELEMENTS*

It is helpful to view specific examples of tiered instruction. The learning experiences that follow incorporate tiered elements to vary core curriculum tasks in response to the assessed readiness of the students participating in station-based learning. Sometimes only one element from the continuum of complexity needs to be selected to appropriately vary a learning task. The following learning experience is tiered by using only one tiered element.

> ### Example: Tier a reading station by resources.
>
> To develop fluency skills, the reading station provides tiered resources by including fiction and nonfiction print at different readability levels. All students select which print to read as they practice fluency skills and time their own reading rate.

While tiering by a single element is possible, tiered elements are often interdependent. Most tiered learning experiences result from a combination of several elements working together to appropriately vary complexity and promote all students' continuous learning.

> ### Example: Tier a math station by background knowledge and skills, resources, support system, and complexity of product.
>
> Provide background information resources at two different levels of readability for student reference, have a special education assistant available to support two special-need students at the station, and tier the product assignments. Specifically, the three product options that follow are tiered with simple to more complex applications. It is important to note, however, that all of the product tasks are designed to require higher-level thinking and are interesting tasks that appeal to students.
> - ✓ Option 1. Students toss a number cube and then see how many division problems they can produce with that number as the quotient.
> - ✓ Option 2. Students use manipulatives and devise a process by which they might teach division to a younger child.
> - ✓ Option 3. One student writes a test with complex word problems that other students might complete to demonstrate that they know, understand, and are able to use division.

Kingore, B. (2011). *Tiered Learning Stations in Minutes*. Austin, TX: PA Publishing.

## STEPS IN DEVELOPING TIERED LEARNING EXPERIENCES FOR STATIONS

> Differentiation challenges educators to design learning experiences
> that enable all learners to experience continuous learning.
> *Not too hard, not too easy, just right.*

In tiered learning stations, provide varied levels of activities to ensure that students explore ideas at levels that build upon what they already know and facilitate their continued progression. To develop tiered learning experiences, begin with tasks from the core curriculum and identify which of the six tiered elements best relate to potential learning in that station. Scan the tiered elements continuum to select one or more appropriate applications that range from simpler to more complex and match the assessed backgrounds of the students. Use those selected applications to vary the learning tasks in the core curriculum. Review the learning tasks to ensure that each variation is mentally engaging, targets

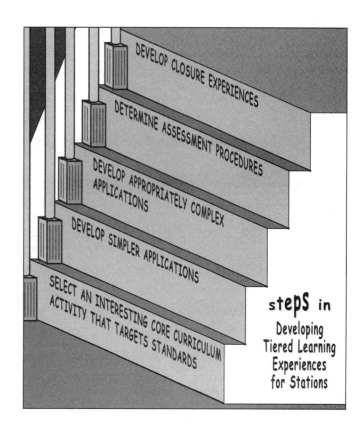

essential concepts and skills, and is planned to enable students to experience success. Activities that engage students slightly beyond what they find easy or comfortable provide genuine challenge and contribute to achievement gains.

## *Step 1*

*Select a core curriculum activity that targets key concepts or skills, is interesting, and appropriately challenges most students.*

> **Core Curriculum:** Targeting the skills of character analysis, cause and effect, and sequence, students use a Two-Column Chart or T-Chart to list in sequence the cause and effect of events involving the protagonist.

Kingore, B. (2011). *Tiered Learning Stations in Minutes*. Austin, TX: PA Publishing.

## Step 2

*Use simpler applications to vary the task appropriately for students with fewer skills.*

> **Tiered Elements:** *Resource.* Provide multiple novels that range from below to above grade level readability with similar themes and well-crafted characters. *Structure of the process.* Provide a Two-Column Chart with the effects of the events listed in random order on one side of the chart. Students determine each cause and reorder the events in sequence. *Support system.* Students work in pairs to discuss and complete the task.

## Step 3

*Adapt the task's complexity for students ready for heightened challenge.*

> **Tiered Elements:** *Resource.* Provide novels at readability levels that are beyond grade level, have similar themes, and include well-crafted characters. *Structure of the process* and *complexity of the product.*
>
> Option 1. Pairs of students use a Two-Column Chart to compare the main character at the beginning and end of the book. They determine the events that caused the character to change and then organize those events in sequence.
>
> Option 2. Individually, students create a Venn diagram comparing the main characters in each of the two novels they read. Then, two or three students compare their Venn diagrams and identify how those traits caused similar or different effects in the sequence of both stories.

## Step 4

*Determine appropriate assessment and evaluation procedures to document that each student learns the targeted concepts and skills.*

> **Example:** In station logs, students write how they used the skills of character analysis, cause and effect, and sequence in their product. Additionally, students must be prepared to orally explain applications of those skills to any adult or peer who asks. Students use a rubric to self-assess the quality of their product before posting it or turning it in for adult evaluation.

Kingore, B. (2011). *Tiered Learning Stations in Minutes.* Austin, TX: PA Publishing.

# Step 5

*Develop appropriate closure experiences to share through whole class instruction.*

> **Example:** As station time finishes, one member of each station is randomly selected
> to orally summarize the work at that station with the rest of the class.

## 38 QUICK WAYS TO TIER LEARNING TASKS

Consider the examples on Figures 3.2 and 3.3 for efficient ways to tier the complexity of learning experiences. The suggestions are intended to be generalizable and apply to multiple grade levels, different content areas, and a variety of topics. While these suggestions do not encompass the entire spectrum of tiered elements, they do enable several efficient and effective adaptations to the core curriculum. In a classroom with a range of mixed-readiness levels, students benefit from the alternative ways to learn, and teachers advance with small steps toward tiered applications.

***Caution!*** Avoid reverting to simple levels of thinking as a way to simplify tasks. Learning is more engaging and long-term when high levels of thinking are employed as often as possible with all students.

***Caution!*** When using less complex text, affirm that the provided information and content vocabulary remains viable rather than risk dumbing-down the learning experience.

Kingore, B. (2011). *Tiered Learning Stations in Minutes*. Austin, TX: PA Publishing.

• Figure 3.2 •
# Quick Ways to Tier Learning Tasks for Struggling Learners

**Check potential applications**

❏  Organize mixed-ability groupings so peers support each other.

❏  Group a fluent bilingual student with a student learning English.

❏  Use an aide or other adult to increase individual attention.

❏  Make student task assistants available to intervene as needed.

❏  Provide a recording of directions or explanations of skills that students revisit as needed.

❏  Assign fewer problems or less lengthy text so students can devote more time to processing data.

❏  Invite two or three peers to complete the task together.

❏  Include a manipulative that makes the task more concrete.

❏  Provide word banks.

❏  Provide a graphic organizer as a guide to help students process information.

❏  Structure the process by supplying a list of subparts or a template with sentence starters to guide thinking and organization.

❏  Supply grade-level resources with the main points and key terms highlighted.

❏  Use grade-level vocabulary in directions and content.

❏  Invite students to draw or quick sketch examples to illustrate and support their understanding.

❏  Use products that are familiar.

❏  Use a process that is concrete and requires a minimum number of steps.

❏  Identify and list the steps in a process for students to refer to as they implement the process.

❏  Locate examples for key content points in below-level or on-grade-level text for student to reference.

❏  Provide computer software that allows a range of levels and an individualized pace for learning.

Kingore, B. (2011). *Tiered Learning Stations in Minutes*. Austin, TX: PA Publishing.

• Figure 3.3 •

# *Quick Ways to Tier Learning Tasks to Increase Complexity*

**Check potential applications**

❑ Occasionally, place two or more advanced students together at the same station to pursue content depth with increased rigor.

❑ Challenge two or three peers to work together using beyond grade-level materials to complete a more in-depth version of the task.

❑ Expect individuals to complete the task without assistance.

❑ Assign an individual or pair to produce an original example for others to use.

❑ Direct an individual or pair to produce high-level questions for others to research.

❑ Invite an individual or pair to plan a Socratic Seminar on the topic.

❑ Rather than actually completing the task, students analyze the process and write a *how-to* explaining the step-by-step procedure that would complete the task.

Appropriately stimulate the level of challenge by inviting or requiring students to:

❑ Produce original graphic organizers that process and organize the information.

❑ Incorporate professional-level vocabulary whenever possible.

❑ Reach consensus regarding the five words most essential to the topic.

❑ Use computer technology to develop graphics that synthesize data.

❑ Interview professionals to determine how the targeted academic skills are required in professional fields.

❑ Investigate issues and ethics related to current topics.

❑ Explore multiple perspectives that differ from the point of view presented in the text.

❑ Investigate the topic across time: past, present, and future trends.

❑ Summarize the process or data with words and symbols

❑ Write a test covering the content for others to complete.

❑ Use advanced resources to support or refute a list of key content points.

❑ Use computer software that allows a higher range of skill and content levels with an individualized pace for learning.

Kingore, B. (2011). *Tiered Learning Stations in Minutes*. Austin, TX: PA Publishing.

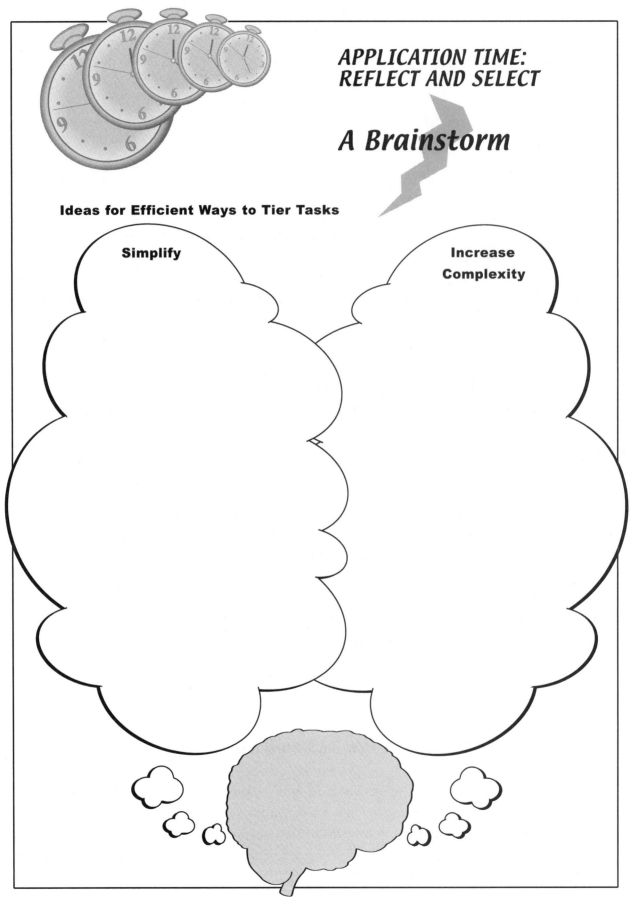

## APPLICATION TIME: REFLECT AND SELECT

## A Brainstorm

**Ideas for Efficient Ways to Tier Tasks**

Simplify

Increase Complexity

Kingore, B. (2011). *Tiered Learning Stations in Minutes*. Austin, TX: PA Publishing.

# • 4 •
# Twenty Plus Twelve Tiered Learning Stations in Minutes

The plans that follow are ideas for the kinds of tiered learning stations that enable teachers to make the most efficient use of their instruction time while providing significant learning experiences for all students. The learning applications for each station are posed as examples to prompt teachers' decisions of the specific learning experiences that would best apply to their curricula and learning standards as well as respond to students' capabilities and interests.

The plans do not include the lists of curricula skills and concepts at each station since most of those specific skills and concepts vary by grade level, content area, and topic. Instead, teachers refer to their learning standards or to the Common Core State Standards (2010) in order to determine the essential academic skills to incorporate at each station. As a guide, the Tool Box CD includes examples of content learning standards and how to display these skills at a station.

Nevertheless, certain communication skills, social interaction skills, and thinking skills are germane to all learning stations and continuously apply as students work and learn. Consequently, these skills help focus learning priorities and provide important information to students and observers. Convey these skills through one or more of five options:

- Post the skills at each station,
- Organize the skills on one class poster,
- Include a list of the skills in students' station logs,
- Share the skills in a written letter to parents, and/or
- Post the skills on the class web page.

## STATION SKILLS:
## COMMUNICATION, SOCIAL INTERACTION, AND THINKING

Communication skills, social interaction skills, and thinking skills are interdependent and rarely used independently of one another. While there are numerous related skills, those listed here are frequently noted for their direct impact on achievement. They are presented in alphabetical order to avoid implying a hierarchy of significance. Use the list as a substantiation of the value of learning stations or as a checklist to skim when developing a list of skills to share and post.

Kingore, B. (2011). *Tiered Learning Stations in Minutes*. Austin, TX: PA Publishing.

## COMMUNICATION SKILLS

### Nonverbal

- Body language and gestures
- Encouragement
- Inference and interpretation
- Listening
- Observation

### Reading

- Communication
- Context clues
- Critical analysis
- Directions
- Inference and interpretation
- Substantiation within text

### Verbal

- Clarification
- Description
- Directions
- Elaboration
- Explanation

### Vocabulary

- Academic terminology
- Incisiveness
- Multisyllabic words
- Spelling

## SOCIAL INTERACTION

- Conflict resolution
- Cooperation
- Leadership
- Patience
- Problem solving
- Sportsmanship
- Comprehension of others' perspective

## THINKING SKILLS

### Classification

- Analogies
- Attribute analysis
- Categorization

- Cause and effect
- Patterning

### Comparative Reasoning

- Fact and opinion
- Identification of ambiguity
- Point of view
- Reality and fantasy
- Sequence
- Similarities and differences

### Evaluative Reasoning

- Decision making
- Establishment and application of criteria
- Judgment
- Logical conclusion
- Logical consequences
- Probability
- Ranking or prioritization
- Relevancy
- Substantiation
- Relationships

### Inference

- Assumption
- Generalization
- Hypothesis
- Interpretation
- Prediction

### Inquiry

- Analysis
- Deductive thinking
- Formulation
- Inductive thinking
- Interpretation
- Investigation
- Problem solving

### Organization

- Analysis
- Planning
- Sequential order
- Summarization
- Synthesis

Kingore, B. (2011). *Tiered Learning Stations in Minutes*. Austin, TX: PA Publishing.

## 20 PLANS FOR TIERED LEARNING STATIONS

The plans that follow provide an overview of high-interest, low-preparation learning stations that teachers can quickly implement to involve students in practicing and extending skills and concepts in different content areas and topics. The intent of the plans is to promote teachers' thinking about their students' interests and capabilities and how to best use learning stations to foster students' continuous learning of essential concepts and skills.

Each learning station plan includes suggested grade levels, tiered elements, a brief overview of the station, equipment or material needs, and several examples of learning experiences and applications. In general, the tasks are tiered from more simple to more complex throughout each learning station or within each skill area. The learning experiences are intended to be helpful suggestions but not necessarily sufficient to complete a station that continues over an extended period of time. Use these examples to foster thinking of the kinds and levels of tiered learning experiences applicable to multiple content areas and specific students' capabilities. Add topic-related items to each station as appropriate to keep the stations relevant and timely.

Some equipment is common to all or most stations. Examples of general equipment and materials are listed here rather than repeated for each station.

- Icons and signs to represent each station's topic or theme
- Desks or tables and chairs
- Writing utensils in a variety of colors and forms to increase visual appeal
- Paper as appropriate to the learning tasks and age of the children
- Nonpermanent adhesive for posting products on walls, windows, and cabinets
- Markers or crayons, Cray-Pas™, unlined copy paper, paste sticks, scissors, and tape

Many stations include tiered task cards delineating a variety of learning tasks. Task cards detail learning experiences that students complete without direct teacher instruction. The tasks must be designed so they are relevant, interesting, and incorporate important learning experiences that target concepts and skills tiered to the varied readiness levels in a classroom.

> Refer to the learning station problems and possible solutions in Chapter 10 for suggestions regarding how to code the levels of tiered tasks and how to monitor the specific level that students select.

Kingore, B. (2011). *Tiered Learning Stations in Minutes*. Austin, TX: PA Publishing.

# *Breaking News! Learn All About It!*

**Grade Levels: K-8**

**Tiered Factors:**

- Background knowledge and skills
- Support system
- Concrete or abstract thinking
- Resources
- Complexity of product

This station focuses on current events inside and outside of the classroom. It is a place where students share personal news or comment on current issues in the news. The objective is to provide authentic reasons to read and write as well as to maintain interest in current affairs that affect students.

## Equipment/Material

- Current magazines and newspapers with stories of students' interests at varied readability levels
- White board, bulletin board, or cork board
- Free-standing photograph frame
- Computer (optional)

## Learning Experiences

- **Notes**

  Invite students to write and post notes to one another on a board or class blog. Conduct a class discussion in which the group analyzes the advantages and potential disadvantages of posting notes and then problem solve how to make this opportunity a valued and interactive class learning experience. Emphasize that all notes must be positive in tone and be sensitive to insuring that every class member receives notes. When necessary, suggest to one student to write a note to a particular student or occasionally write a note from teacher to student.

- **Personal Announcements**

  Individual students write, illustrate, and post announcements such as a personal accomplishment, a new baby in the family, or a recognition outside of class.

Kingore, B. (2011). *Tiered Learning Stations in Minutes*. Austin, TX: PA Publishing.

- **Photograph Frame**

  Invite students to place an important article, personal reflection, or announcement in a stand-up photograph frame at the station. The intent is to emphasize the importance of the item by providing a showcase that calls attention to the information.

- **Current Events**

  Students read provided newspapers or articles about current events of interest to the class. They also post announcements of upcoming events of interest to the class.

- **Political or Current Event Cartoons**

  Visual, spatial students draw and post cartoons depicting current events or their perception of political events.

- **Comparative Thinking**

  Provide articles about a sports event of high-interest to the students. Insure that one of the write ups is from a local paper and another is from the opposing team's area paper. In pairs, have students compare the articles and list three or more occasions where specific words or phrases affect the slant of the information.

- **Perspective or Propaganda**

  Post a thought-provoking article for students to review. Include questions to promote students' high-level thinking while remaining sensitive to students' own perspectives. Allow students to work together or individually to respond to the questions.

  > *How do the word choices in this article attempt to influence your thinking?*
  > *Which word choices reveal the perspective of the author of this article?*
  > *What do you find most provocative about this article?*

- **Issues and Ethics**

  Near a current event or news article, post questions that foster students' reactions.

  > *So what do you think about it?*
  > *What would you do?*
  > *What would you want to change?*

  Students write or record their reflections on issues and ethics relating to this event. Challenge them to include support for their ideas and document sources as often as possible. Encourage students to create ongoing communications about current events and engage in comparative thinking by adding written responses to each other's reflections. Many students have opinions and relevant conclusions to share if only someone seeks their perspectives.

Kingore, B. (2011). *Tiered Learning Stations in Minutes*. Austin, TX: PA Publishing.

## Cereal Box Sensations

**Grade Levels:  K-8**

**Tiered Factors:**

- Background knowledge and skills
- Structure or complexity of the process
- Concrete or abstract thinking
- Complexity of product

Cereal boxes are a dominant and highly-recognizable component of Western culture. They are visually appealing and frequently read by children and adults alike. Cereal Box Sensations uses this motivational form of print to integrate a myriad of learning experiences. While skill connections are numerous with this station, a sampling of activities across the curriculum serve to prompt further applications.

### Equipment/Material

- A wide variety of empty cereal boxes
- Paper plates or napkins
- Task cards of tiered learning experiences for students to select and complete

### Learning Experiences

- **Primary Math Applications**

    Have children work on a napkin or plate for cleanliness.

    ✓ Counting

    Children measure out one-fourth cup of cereal, count the number of pieces, and write that number. They then regroup the pieces in pairs, count those sets, write that number, and write how many are left over. Finally, they can eat the cereal.

    *I counted _____ pieces of cereal. I made _____ pairs. I have _____ left over.*

    ✓ Classifying

    Children measure out one-fourth cup of cereal. They sort, draw, and list how many ways they can classify the cereal pieces before eating the cereal.

    ✓ Sets

    Children measure out one-fourth cup of cereal. They divide the cereal pieces into sets and arrange the sets from one piece through as many complete sets as they can make. They write what they accomplished before eating the cereal.

> *I made sets from 1 to _____. I have _____ pieces left over.*

✓ Pattern

Children measure out one-fourth cup of cereal. Using cereal with different colors or shapes, children make a pattern and then draw a copy of their pattern and label it before eating the cereal.

- **Sensational Sentences**
  - ✓ Students write a nine word sentence telling why a cereal is sensational.
  - ✓ Students write a twelve-word sentence that uses the word *cereal* as the fourth word.

- **Math Applications**
  - ✓ Estimation; one-to-one correspondence; subtraction
    Students estimate and record how many pieces they can capture in a one-half cup measuring cup, fill the measuring cup with cereal, count the pieces, and write a math problem showing the difference between their estimate and their actual total.
  - ✓ Averaging
    For three different times, students repeat capturing one-half cup of cereal and determine the average number of pieces in a level one-half cup.
  - ✓ Comparative thinking
    Compare the results of the estimation and averaging learning experiences using a different cereal with pieces of a different size.
  - ✓ Recommended serving size
    Students pour a bowl of cereal that is about the size they usually eat. Using the information on the box, students research the recommended serving size and compare that recommendation to how much they usually eat. What ramifications does that difference have on the calories being consumed? Ask students to measure their preferred serving size and then use math to figure out how many calories they would consume.
  - ✓ Mathematical terminology
    Using as many math terms as possible, students describe the dimensions and attributes of one container without revealing which cereal box they described. They post the results and challenge peers to read the description and correctly identify the box.

- **Map Skills**
  On a large map, students use push pins or sticky-note tabs to mark the locations of several different cereal producers. Then, they select one site and research to determine multiple reasons for its location. For example, they might consider historical context, economic conditions, weather, transportation issues, and family connections.

Kingore, B. (2011). *Tiered Learning Stations in Minutes*. Austin, TX: PA Publishing.

- **Health**

  Students research to determine the cereal with the lowest sugar and highest food value and then find the cereal with the highest sugar and lowest food value. Students write and illustrate a response explaining what factors influenced their decision of the food value of the cereal.

- **Letter Writing**
  - ✓ Students write an email or letter to actually mail to the manufacturer of their favorite cereal. In the letter, they explain the reasons for their opinion, a suggestion for continued improvement, and what action they would like the company to take in response.
  - ✓ Students write an email or letter to actually mail to the manufacturer that makes a cereal they do not like. In the letter, they explain what they find distasteful about the cereal and offer suggestions for improvements that would make the cereal better and more appealing to children. Students conclude by detailing what action they believe the company should take in response to this problem.

- **Survey**
  - ✓ Students survey twenty adults and twenty peers to determine their favorite and least-liked cereals. They ask each person which factors most influence them when selecting cereals.
  - ✓ Students create a list of the *Top 10 Reasons to Select a Cereal*.
  - ✓ Students graph the results of the most and least favorites.
  - ✓ Students analyze what conclusions they might draw from comparing the preferences by age groups.
  - ✓ Students summarize their information to post at the station or on a class blog.

- **Parody**

  Students create a parody of a cereal box by using the format of a particular cereal box to summarize a current event, historical event, story, or novel. What is the name, illustration, and slogan for the cereal parody? Which components, such as characters, dates, and related items, might be interpreted as the nutritional ingredients and the nutritional value? How is the factory location for producing the cereal like the historical setting or setting for the events in the story, and how does that setting influence the plot or the events that unfold? Which features of a cereal box might be used to relate the main ideas of the event or story? Challenge students to see how many aspects of the cereal they can cleverly integrate into the parody. Students then organize the information on a cereal-like box as they incorporate illustrations and logos to complete their product.

Kingore, B. (2011). *Tiered Learning Stations in Minutes*. Austin, TX: PA Publishing.

# Classification Board

**Grade Levels: K-8**

**Tiered Factors:**

- Background knowledge and skills
- Support system
- Resources

Classification is recognized as part of the most effective strategy to increase achievement gains (Marzano, 2004). A Classification Board requires the categorization and comparative thinking skills that lead to understanding the similarities and differences of the varied sub-parts of a topic. The board is easily divided with yarn into two or more areas that provide the organization for categorization. Students use push pins, self-sticking clips, or nonpermanent adhesive to appropriately categorize pictures and small items. The specific examples to classify can be stored in a cup or small box stapled to the bottom corner of the board.

Typically, students work together in small groups. A classification board enables students of all ages to practice and extend a myriad of skills and concepts. Several examples serve to prompt decisions of additional applications across the curriculum.

## Equipment/Material

- Bulletin board
- Yarn or colored masking tape to divide the board into sections
- Push pins, self-sticking clips, or nonpermanent adhesive

## Learning Experiences

- **Categories**
  Increase students' ownership by discussing a topic for a classification board. Facilitate as students determine the most appropriate categories to use on the board to organize that topic and then collect the examples to categorize.

- **Students as Producers**
  Some of the greatest learning value of this station occurs when students prepare the items to classify. Initiate the station by having students write, draw, or cut out the examples

that will be classified. This exercise requires them to analyze the subparts of the whole topic. When an appropriately substantial set of examples is ready, switch the task at the station to having students classify the items.

- **Science**
  ✓ Label each column of a two column board with *Magnets attract these* and *Magnets do not attract these.* Children use nonpermanent adhesive or push pins to classify appropriate real items and related pictures.
  ✓ Divide the board into quadrants and label each with one of the seasons of the year. Children draw pictures, cut out pictures, and write words and sentences related to a season to place in each quadrant.
  ✓ Divide the board into three areas and provide words and pictures for students to classify *Forms of Matter.*
  ✓ Label each column with a different biome. Students classify pictures and strips of cardstock containing attributes under the applicable biome.

- **Language Arts**
  ✓ Grammar
    - Divide the board into two areas labeled nouns and adjectives. Students write words and also draw and label pictures to place in each category.
    - Divide the board into four areas. Students place cut-out words and phrases in the appropriate column for adverbs, adjectives, conjunctions, and interjections.
  ✓ Stories and Novels
    As a summative task, divide the board into multiple sections, each labeled with the title of a story or novel the class has read. For several days, provide index cards on which students list on individual cards a key point or significant detail, such as key words, the author, the illustrator, a sentence about a particular character trait, or sentences that relate key events, problems, solutions, and main ideas of the featured stories and novels. On additional cards, students illustrate key items, scenes, and symbols relevant to one of the stories or novels. When an appropriate set of cards is complete, the task switches from preparation to classification as students use push pins to classify each card by placing it in the section for the particular story or novel.

- **Math**
  ✓ Number and Set
    Post large numerals randomly all about the board. Children post cards with equations or pictures of sets of objects under the appropriate numeral. Provide multiple cards for each numeral to increase the challenge.

Kingore, B. (2011). *Tiered Learning Stations in Minutes*. Austin, TX: PA Publishing.

✓ Math Operations

Divide the board into four areas. Label each of the four areas with a different math operation. Students read provided word problems to place in the column for the operation that is initially required by that problem.

- **Social Studies**
  ✓ Divide the board into areas for different occupations. Children place pictures and words related to occupations in the appropriate area. Some of the pictures might show people in their work uniforms. Other pictures show tools or items used in different jobs. Encourage children to discuss which pictures or words might belong in more than one occupation.
  ✓ Divide the board into columns for regions of the United States. Students analyze and classify a set of attributes according to which are characteristic of a specific region.
  ✓ Students classify cause and effects related to several key historical events.

- **Generalizable Categories**

  Divide the board into areas and post three or more generalizable categories that are applicable to multiple topics, such as *attributes, terminology, examples, non-examples, events,* and *comparisons*. When the topic of study changes, leave the categories, remove the examples the students posted, post the new topic, and proceed with students searching for appropriate examples to post.

 *Caution!* With young children, provide a child-safe, two-step piece of furniture so they can independently reach all of the areas of the bulletin board.

Kingore, B. (2011). *Tiered Learning Stations in Minutes*. Austin, TX: PA Publishing.

# Editors' Office

**Grade Levels: 2-8**

**Tiered Factors:**

*   Background knowledge and skills
*   Support system
*   Complexity of product

The Editors' Office is a station where students are only allowed entrance when they have work to edit or revise. The emphasis is on authentic editing or revision opportunities in which students reflect upon their own writing rather than contrived composition exercises.

To add to the aura of being special, the area is purposely kept small with room for one or two students. This elite atmosphere adds appeal to an often unpopular task. Basic routines such as turning on the lamp and putting on a visor add appeal to the station and help some students settle into the writing process. The simple pleasure of a special location where only the editor can select special pens and use professional editors' symbols increases students' enthusiasm to bring their written drafts to the station.

## Equipment/Material

*   Desk
*   Lamp
*   Editor Visor
*   Editing forms
*   Editing bookmarks
*   Thesaurus
*   Word book for quick spelling checks
*   Writing style handbook to resolve usage questions
*   A variety of pens in different shapes and in different bright colors
*   Photograph of an editor at work; an older, historical view is often appealing

## Learning Experiences

*   **Sign-up List**

    Add a sign-up list to this station as it attracts students who typically do not like to edit or revise their work.

Kingore, B. (2011). *Tiered Learning Stations in Minutes.* Austin, TX: PA Publishing.

- **Editing Symbols**

Students refer to the posted editing marks to use when editing one of their written compositions.

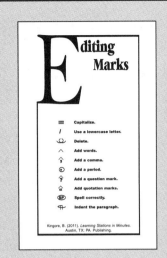

- **Revision Checklist**

Students refer to specifically checked elements on a revision checklist and emphasize those elements when revising their work. Accenting a few elements helps students focus on specific aspects of revision and seems less overwhelming to many writers. The Tool Box CD includes a full-sized example of a revision checklist.

- **Peer Editors**

When support is needed, invite two students to work at the station together. They begin by editing and revising a written piece from one of the two students. Then, they peer edit and revise a work by the second student.

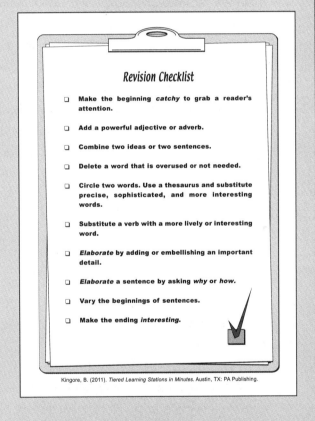

- **Authors as Models**

Invite students to post statements and revelations from successful authors that substantiate how editing and revision is a crucial part of publishing. For example, Helen Lester, in her autobiographical picture book *Author: A True Story,* humorously shows multiple revisions of a paragraph as she strives to make it more effective. She laments how she goes over the work again and again, with little changes here and there, until it has to be printed, and then it's too late!

Kingore, B. (2011). *Tiered Learning Stations in Minutes.* Austin, TX: PA Publishing.

## Error Analysis Station

**Grade Levels: 1-8**

**Tiered Factors:**

* Background knowledge and skills
* Structure or complexity of the process
* Concrete or abstract thinking

The Error Analysis Station presents information, products, or math problems riddled with mistakes. This content interests students because, as many teachers have observed, students are often more interested in diagnosing other people's mistakes than their own. This station offers an appealing way to call attention to skill errors without pinning negative associations on specific students.

The station contains a number of flawed examples representing the range of mistakes students are demonstrating with a current skill or concept. Collect a representative set of errors by reviewing students' class and home work. Include a range of skill levels and tier the tasks to enable all students to experience continuous learning. Copy each error on a separate index card, and include eight to twelve tiered cards in the station. When working at the station, students select a card and use the applicable error analysis form to scaffold their thinking and record their responses. Full sized templates for these forms are included on the Tool Box CD.

All students complete error analysis cards one or more times a week. The cards can be used multiple times by different students who need to practice that specific need. At the end of one or two weeks, update the stations' content by removing the cards that are no longer relevant and adding a few new cards that extend the learning applications.

Error correction is an important feedback function that helps students with self-regulation of learning by promoting their understanding of the learning goal, how close current work

### Error Analysis

NAME _____                ERROR ANALYSIS CARD #: _____

Copy the sentence here.

What is incorrect in this information?

How can the error be corrected?

Kingore, B. (2011). *Tiered Learning Stations in Minutes.* Austin, TX: PA Publishing.

Kingore, B. (2011). *Tiered Learning Stations in Minutes.* Austin, TX: PA Publishing.

comes to it, and what they should do next (Hattie & Timperley, 2007). Inasmuch as these are three crucial components of the formative assessment cycle, the Error Analysis Station becomes a significant assessment tool.

### Equipment/Material

✎ Index cards
✎ Math Error Analysis forms
✎ Error Analysis forms

### Learning Experiences

- **Math Error Analysis**

**Math Error Analysis**

NAME _Samantha_                                    ERROR ANALYSIS CARD #: _13_

| Copy the problem here. | What is incorrect in this problem? |
|---|---|
| $x + 2 - 3x + 4 = 0$ | _Negative numbers are not applied correctly_ |
| $-4x = 6$ | **How can the error be corrected?** |
| $x = \frac{-6}{4}$ | _First, when two and four are added, they equal six on the left side of the equation and_ <u>_negative_</u> _six on the right. Then, x - 3x does not equal -4x. It equals -2x._ |
| $x = -1\frac{1}{2}$ | _The correct answer is 3._ |

Kingore, B. (2011). *Tiered Learning Stations in Minutes.* Austin, TX: PA Publishing.

Peruse students' classroom work and homework papers to collect math problems with errors. Select problems that represent the levels of difficulty appropriate for the readiness range in the class and contain errors that correspond to one or more students' practice needs. Secure a selection of problems that represent the difficulties students typically experience when learning current skills and concepts. Number several index cards and copy a flawed problem on each so the cards are in an adult's handwriting and do not risk revealing which student made the error.

Students respond to an error card by completing a Math Error Analysis form on which they write their name, the number of the card they review, the problem, and a few descriptive sentences that answer the following questions:

*What is incorrect in this problem?*
*How can the error be corrected?*

All students complete error analysis cards one or more times a week. The cards can be used multiple times by different students assessed with that specific need. At the end of one or two weeks, update the stations' content by removing the cards that are no longer relevant and adding a few new cards that extend the learning applications.

The difficulty level of the problems on the Math Error Analysis cards can range from simple math operations to pre-algebra concepts. Since the cards are tiered with problems that vary in complexity, teachers either challenge students to select a problem at their level or assign students which cards to complete.

Kingore, B. (2011). *Tiered Learning Stations in Minutes.* Austin, TX: PA Publishing.

- ### Language Arts Error Analysis

This application is similar to the math error analysis but focuses on language arts skills and concepts. Typical errors are collected from students' class work and homework. When a reoccurring error is detected, teachers write the text that includes the flawed example on a numbered index card or half-sheet of paper.

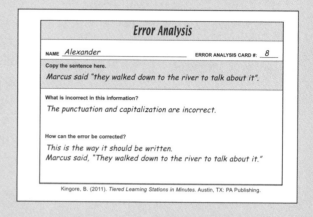

Include eight to twelve tiered cards in the station. Students select a card and complete an Error Analysis form on which they write their name and the number of the card they review. They copy the flawed sentence and write a few descriptive sentences that answer the following questions:

*What is incorrect in this information?*

*How can the error be corrected?*

- ### Memorization Error Analysis

This application is useful when students are required to memorize information such as the Declaration of Independence, science or math formulas, or a poem. On large numbered index cards or half-sheets of paper, copy the information but substitute errors for some of the accurate data. Prepare several cards with different errors and laminate the cards. Students use wipe off pens to correct the copy, check their changes with the original information, and write a goal for what they will do next to continue learning. They then wipe off their editing marks for the next student.

Kingore, B. (2011). *Tiered Learning Stations in Minutes*. Austin, TX: PA Publishing.

## Expert Quests

**Grade Levels: K-8**

**Tiered Factors:**

- Background knowledge and skills
- Structure or complexity of the process
- Concrete or abstract thinking
- Complexity of product

This is a student-developed learning station that establishes a peer audience for student projects and research. Expert Quests highlights products from students' individual pursuits, interest-based research, and small group projects. The station provides an authentic audience for students' work, enables peers to participate in classmates' learning, and fosters peer understanding that classmates not only have valuable and interesting information to share but may also be in-house experts on certain topics. Expert Quests promotes higher achievement by honoring students' interests and individual talents. Some students are clearly motivated to work more intently toward developing a high-level product when their work has an audience.

Provide a corner in the classroom that students organize to showcases their projects. The station changes as different students develop additional products. Increase student ownership by involving the class in determining how long a product remains at the station and eliciting their ideas regarding display possibilities. For example, nonpermanent adhesives enable students to post items on the walls; bookshelves or stacked boxes provide places for three-dimensional items.

This station should emphasize in-depth content and interpretation rather than flashy production. Many simple presentation formats are possible so that even young students can experience the satisfaction of creating a display. Each project should include a visual aid or graphic, one or more essential questions of the project, and interactive elements for classmates to experience as they learn about the project. When appropriate, challenge students to develop a rubric for peers to evaluate the product.

Kingore, B. (2011). *Tiered Learning Stations in Minutes*. Austin, TX: PA Publishing.

**Equipment/Material**

   Student products

   Nonpermanent adhesives

**Learning Experiences**

**Simple Products**

- **Audio tape**

  Children record themselves reading aloud an informative book about their topic of interest. They include their own narrative to embellish and customize the information with additional details they know from their research.

- **Collage poster**

  The visual student makes a collage of drawings, cut-out illustrations, symbols, and words significant to the topic. Under each item is a paper flap with a key word or provocative question on it. Peers lift each flap to learn more information.

- **Flap books**

  Students fold paper to create a flap book with an essential question on the outside of each flap. Peers lift a flap to reveal the answer and references to materials in the station that provide additional information, illustrations, and unexpected connections about that question.

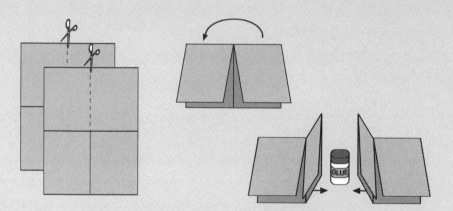

- **Scavenger hunt**

  The hunt begins with one or more posted questions about a topic. Six to ten descriptive cards then lead the reader from one resource in the station to another in search of the multiple components of the answers to the essential questions.

Kingore, B. (2011). *Tiered Learning Stations in Minutes*. Austin, TX: PA Publishing.

- **Shape books**

  Shape books are book with pages cut in a shape related to the content. Students determine a shape or symbol to represent their research topic and cut several pages in that shape to use as the paper for writing their research results.

**More Sophisticated Products**

- **Trivia game**

  Students develop a set of informative cards with questions and detailed responses that progress in difficulty about the topic. They organize the cards into a trivia game for other students to play at the novice, student, or scholar level.

- **PowerPoint™**

  Students organize a PowerPoint™ presentation so others may learn about the topic.

- **Digital photographs**

  A student creates a photo essay with photographs and large index cards containing explanations, such as *The Construction of the Children's Art Museum.*

- **Debate video**

  Two to four students collaboratively research an issue or ethical concern. They videotape their information and conclusions in a debate format that presents two or more viewpoints.

- **Website**

  Students produce a website to showcase their information, use hyperlinks to create flow and organization, and guide others to learn about their topic.

Kingore, B. (2011). *Tiered Learning Stations in Minutes.* Austin, TX: PA Publishing.

# Games Galore

**Grade Levels: K-8**

**Tiered Factors:**

- Background knowledge and skills
- Support system
- Structure or complexity of the process

Academic games appeal to and benefit very young learners through middle school scholars. Locate this station in a corner or at a book shelf containing a collection of board and strategy games that children play to apply content area concepts and skills.

There are appropriate commercial game choices for all age groups that foster the practice and extension of skills and concepts. Analyze potential skill and concept applications, and select those games that incorporate essential concepts and skills or relate to the current topic of study. Possible examples include a variety of card games and a range of board games from Candy Land to Pictionary to Scrabble to chess. Inasmuch as the station is based on commercial games, preparation of this station is quickly accomplished by designating a small area in the classroom and placing a small number of games in that area.

Research studies confirm that using academic games in the classroom increases achievement gains and builds academic vocabulary. However, games that fail to focus on essential academic content have little effect on student achievement and waste valuable classroom time (Marzano, 2010). The most efficient way to foster academic connections to current topics of study is to organize games around terms and phrases significant to the field of study. Additionally, students experience the greatest enjoyment when the game process is fun competition rather than a high-stakes winner-loser designation.

## Equipment/Material

- Commercial card games and board games with academic applications
- List of websites with academic games
- Computer access (optional)
- Student-developed games

Kingore, B. (2011). *Tiered Learning Stations in Minutes*. Austin, TX: PA Publishing.

### Learning Experiences

* **Games**

  Provide a small number of different card and board games appropriate to the readiness levels of the students. A pair of students selects a game and reads the directions before playing. Require students to reorganize and carefully put the game away to avoid misplacing pieces.

* **Reflection**

  Require students to debrief when the game is finished to elicit their perceptions and extend the learning.

* **Skill analysis**

  Engage students in analyzing the communication skills, social interaction skills, and thinking skills listed as potential skills at all stations to determine which ones they practiced during their interactive game.

* **Flexible thinking, adaptability, and complexity**

  Enhance the level of challenge and content connections at this learning station by extending students' high-level thinking beyond only playing the game. Challenge them to devise rule changes that necessitate high-level thinking, involve a great need for attention, or require a more complex process. Examples of student-created rule changes follow.

  ✓ Use a timer and decrease the time by five seconds for each round of play.

  ✓ Players sit in a circle with a different game on either side. They play two games simultaneously with two different people.

  ✓ When playing Scrabble and other word games, only words with two or more syllables can be scored.

  ✓ Play checkers, chess or Othello with four people instead of two. The two people on each team are not allowed to talk to each other to explain moves or objectives. They must observe and infer intentions.

* **Creativity and In-depth Content**

  Invite students to adapt commercial games to create a new game that is specific to the current topic of study yet extends beyond basic information. For example, three middle school students used the Monopoly game board to develop a game about Egypt with Egyptian sites on the board and cards that related to historical people, events, and the causes and effects of change over time. Provide students with a guide for developing their

Kingore, B. (2011). *Tiered Learning Stations in Minutes*. Austin, TX: PA Publishing.

game, such as the Design-an-Academic-Game guideline shown here. The Tool Box CD includes a full-sized template.

- **Websites**
  - ✓ Post a short list of approved websites that are sources of games with academic connections. Individual students elect to explore and experience one or more of the sites.
  - ✓ Invite students to propose additional sites they find that offer appropriate games with skill applications. To propose a site, a student writes a proposal explaining the academic value of the site and includes reasons why classmates will benefit from the site. A class committee and the teacher review the proposal and research the site before it is added to the recommended list.

- **Evaluation graph**

  Post a large graph with recommended websites and games as the column headings. List the name of each student as a row heading. When a student plays one of the games or uses one of the game websites, that student rates the enjoyment of that experience on a continuum of one to five, with one being low and five being high. Over time, use the results to determine the continued use of each game or site. Students are often interested in and influenced by peer evaluations.

---

### Design-an-Academic-Game

Develop a board game for this topic: _____
Integrate the following skills into the game:

- _____   - _____
- _____   - _____
- _____   - _____

Write the game objectives, rules, and directions in complete sentences and number the directions. Add art, graphics, elaborate fonts, and color to to make the game more attractive and appealing.

Check to be certain to include:

- The name and icon or illustration for the game
- Clearly developed directions
- A game board
- Choice or consequence cards
- Game pieces
- Dice or a spinner

Determine which criteria are most relevant to the product, and develop a rubric to evaluate the effectiveness of the game. Sample criteria include the following.

- Clarity of directions
- Integration of skills
- Quality and depth of content
- Appearance
- Appeal
- _____   - _____
- _____   - _____

Embellish and extend these criteria as appropriate to the work. Then, develop three or four levels of proficiency for each criterion to complete the rubric.

Kingore, B. (2011). *Tiered Learning Stations in Minutes*. Austin, TX: PA Publishing.

---

Kingore, B. (2011). *Tiered Learning Stations in Minutes*. Austin, TX: PA Publishing.

## *Graffiti Board*

**Grade Levels: 2-8**

**Tiered Factors:**

- Background knowledge and skills
- Structure or complexity of the process
- Concrete or abstract thinking
- Resources

The intent of this bulletin board station is to invite students to read and learn about a featured topic. Challenge students to seek interesting ideas that are important to the topic and write on the board, in graffiti style, the significant information they learned so they share it with others. Cover a bulletin board with a light-colored background and topic-related border. Complete the bulletin board with a compelling caption about the current topic of study, such as *What's Significant about the Water Cycle?* Toss a few pillows and clipboards below it, and provide a wide range of topic-related, nonfiction materials. If possible, provide internet access and post a list of interesting, related websites for initiating research.

### Equipment/Material

- Bulletin board
- Clipboards and pillows
- Topic-related, nonfiction books and articles
- Computer and internet access, if possible
- List of websites with related academic connections

### Learning Experiences

- **Resources**

  Provide on grade level, below grade level, and beyond grade level reading materials about the topic. Differentiated resources allow all children to learn at their highest readiness level.

- **Validation**

  Students autograph their information as they post it. This action gives credit to the child who wrote the idea, invites students to further discuss ideas with the author, and encourages others to write information so they are noticed positively for their thinking and research.

Kingore, B. (2011). *Tiered Learning Stations in Minutes*. Austin, TX: PA Publishing.

- **Internet**
  - ✓ If students use information found on the internet, require them to include the website's reference. Utilize this opportunity to discuss the importance of being discriminating about information that is posted on the internet.
  - ✓ Invite students to propose additional websites as they discover significant resources about the topic. To propose a site, a student writes a proposal explaining the academic value of the site and how classmates will benefit. A class committee and the teacher review the proposal and research the site before it is added to the recommended list.

- **Graph**

  Post a graph listing each provided information source or website as a column heading. List student names as the row headings and encourage students to use a continuum of one to five, with five being the highest rating, to rate the interest level and value of each resource they read. Peers are interested in other students' opinions.

- **In-depth Information**

  Challenge students to find information that is new to other students and adult observers. This provocation promotes more content depth from some students and encourages advanced students to pursue beyond grade-level resources.

- **Bibliographic References**

  Students use a standard bibliographic referencing format to list the resource(s) they used so others can find that resource if they are interested in reading further. This referencing also serves to require students to document where they located information.

- **Analogies**

  Challenge students to create and post analogies that respond to the topic. Analogies foster students' high-level thinking and reveal their perception and depth of information.

- **Synthesis**

  Ask students to conclude which three words they believe to be most significant to this topic. Students write their three words on the board, autograph their list, and must be prepared to explain their thinking so others can understand.

 *Idea!* As a simple mnemonic device for young students or students inexperienced with reference formats, teach them *AT-CD* which stands for *Author, Title, Company, Date*. Students reference their graffiti entry by writing the AT-CD facts underneath their information.

Kingore, B. (2011). *Tiered Learning Stations in Minutes*. Austin, TX: PA Publishing.

# *Grocery Store*

**Grade Levels: K-6**

**Tiered Factors:**

- Background knowledge and skills
- Support system
- Complexity of product

This station requires a wide collection of items typically found at a grocery store for students to role play purchasing groceries. The objective is a hands-on, high-interest application of math skills and operations, but a few language arts skills can also be incorporated. To expedite preparation, have students collect and bring to school empty boxes, wrappers, and cans from home.

## Equipment/Material

- Shelves for displaying grocery items, such as empty boxes, wrappers, and cans
- Note pads for writing grocery lists
- Cash register or printing calculator; price labels; play money or blank checks
- Recyclable grocery bags–particularly those with straps for handles

## Learning Experiences

- **Organization**

  Students apply valuable skills as they set up the store. Foster student ownership in this station by having students decide which items to use and how to organize and display those items. Involve them in using grocery ads in newspapers to research the price of each item.

- **Role Play**

  Students elect to role play the store employees or the customers buying groceries.

- **K-1 Grocery Store**

  Price all of the items in whole coin values. Children select items, determine the correct coins, and select the play money coins required to complete their purchases.

- **Grocery Lists**

  Students write grocery lists to follow and check off as they make their purchases.

Kingore, B. (2011). *Tiered Learning Stations in Minutes*. Austin, TX: PA Publishing.

- **Alphabetical Order**
  - ✓ Students arrange all of the grocery items in their store in alphabetical order to expedite others locating specific items.
  - ✓ Using grocery ads in a variety of newspapers, students collaboratively cut out items for each letter of the alphabet to arrange and paste in alphabetical order. Display the chart in the store.

- **Math Operations**
  - ✓ Students purchase three items and figure out the total amount of money they need.
  - ✓ Students randomly draw a price card from a provided set of amounts and determine items to purchase within that budget.
  - ✓ Students randomly draw a price card from a provided set of amounts. They then work to determine the greatest number of items from the store that they would be able to purchase while staying within that budget.
  - ✓ Students determine the cost for non-grocery purchases and then multiply by the rate of sales tax to figure their total cost.
  - ✓ Students write a list of six items they want to purchase. They collect the items, compute the total cost, and then figure out how to divide that total with three friends who will share the items.

- **Grocery Budget Sheets**
  Provide a range of budget sheets that promote students' application of multiple math skills. An example here and in the Tool Box prompts thinking of tasks authentic to current math skills.

- **Make Change**
  Students role play the check out cashier. Using play money, they make change as others pay for their purchases.

- **Health**
  Students write a grocery list that includes items from every area of the food pyramid.

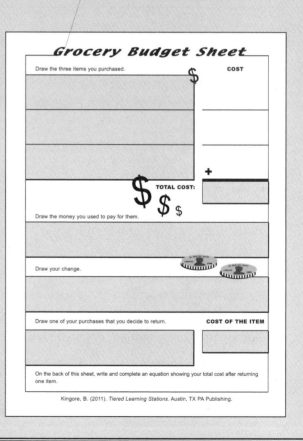

**Grocery Budget Sheet**

Draw the three items you purchased.                    COST

$

TOTAL COST:

+

$ $ $

Draw the money you used to pay for them.

Draw your change.

Draw one of your purchases that you decide to return.     COST OF THE ITEM

On the back of this sheet, write and complete an equation showing your total cost after returning one item.

Kingore, B. (2011). *Tiered Learning Stations*. Austin, TX PA Publishing.

Kingore, B. (2011). *Tiered Learning Stations in Minutes*. Austin, TX: PA Publishing.

# *If the World Were a Village*

**Grade Levels: 3-8**

**Tiered Factors:**

- Background knowledge and skills
- Support system
- Structure or complexity of the process
- Concrete or abstract thinking
- Resources
- Complexity of product

In his book *If the World Were a Village*, David Smith postulates that thinking about our world in terms of the seven billion existing people is too abstract. So he poses to consider the Earth as a village of 100 people and then uses statistics and ratio to convert data. The result is a much more personal and interesting way to look at our world. This station uses social studies, reading, writing, and the math skill of ratio as a device to learn about our global society.

## Equipment/Material

- Smith D. (2002). *If the world were a village.*
- Smith D. (2007). *If the world were a village: Revised.*
- Computer access, if possible for research
- Nonfiction books and articles about countries, states, or cities of interest

## Learning Experiences

- **If the World Were a Village**
  Students read the book and use sticky note tabs to mark data of interest. Encourage students to discuss the statistics they find interesting.

- **If Our School was a Village**
  ✓ Students develop a questionnaire to survey people throughout the school and collect personal and family data. Be sensitive to personal rights and privacy. Monitor the proposed questions for appropriateness, and include questions such as the following.
  *What occupation do you want to have in the future?*
  *Where would you like to visit?*
  *If you could go back in time, which historical person would you want to visit?*

Kingore, B. (2011). *Tiered Learning Stations in Minutes*. Austin, TX: PA Publishing.

*What is your favorite pastime?*

*What is the number of people in your family?*

*How many sisters to you have? How many brothers?*

*How many people in your family know more than one language?*

*What is your family's favorite food?*

✓ Interested students compile and convert the collected data into a village of 100.

✓ Interested students write and illustrate a book for the school that uses the data.

• **State or Community Analysis**

Students use nonfiction materials and the internet to research their state or community. As their research proceeds, they use ratio to covert the statistics they find into the quantity commensurate with a village of 100 people. Students then reflect upon which data most fascinated them when viewed in this manner.

• **Country**

When learning about a different country, have students work individually or in pairs to convert statistics about that country into a village of 100 and then use those results to write, graph, and illustrate a comparison of that country with the similarities and differences of the United States. Require students to note each resource they use to document their data.

• **Comparative Thinking**

Smith wrote a revised version of his book five years after publishing the original. Students read and compare data in the original book with data about the same topic in the revised book. Have them write a record of the changes they found and then predict what trends they foresee based upon these changes.

• **If the World Were a Village Today**

Challenge students to research the most contemporary statistics they can access to determine the current state of our global society.

• **World Watch**

Students bring in articles of interest about events and peoples in the world today to foster discussions of trends and issues from multiple perspectives.

*Idea!* If a student is interested in the task yet lacks the math background to convert the data, allow an older or more experienced math student to help.

Kingore, B. (2011). *Tiered Learning Stations in Minutes*. Austin, TX: PA Publishing.

## In the Real World

**Grade Levels: 3-8**

**Tiered Factors:**

- Background knowledge and skills
- Support system
- Structure or complexity of the process
- Concrete or abstract thinking
- Resources
- Complexity of product

Students often question how the science and math skills or concepts they learn at school relate to the real world. This station invites students to explore content applications through real-life, long-term, interest-based projects collaboratively investigated by individuals or small groups. The projects require the collection of data, more than one step, and multiple solutions. They evolve from students' interests and involve applications of math or science in the real world. The focus is on student inquiry, production, and providing an audience for students' science and math-related interests and research.

### Equipment/Material

- Computer and digital camera
- Fiction and nonfiction resources at diverse readability levels
- List of quality, interactive websites for math and science
- Shelves. Since these products often develop over time, students store work on the shelves with sticky notes to specify work in progress.

### Learning Experiences

- **Investigate**

  Students investigate resources that apply math or science inquiry and problem solving in the real world, such as Ed Zaccaro's *25 Real Life Math Investigations that Will Astound Teachers and Students* or Mark Illingworth's *Real-Life Math Problem Solving.*

- **Cooking Chemistry**

  Students participate in cooking experiences at home or at school to record how many math and science applications they can identify. The focus is how math is required and

Kingore, B. (2011). *Tiered Learning Stations in Minutes*. Austin, TX: PA Publishing.

what chemical reactions occur in common cooking experiences such as making bread, caramel popcorn, and pancakes.

- **Playground Physics**

  Students investigate how many science concepts and principles they can identify on the school playground. They investigate the science concepts and principles applied at an amusement park with rides.

- **Digital photography**
  - ✓ Students take digital photographs of scenes depicting math or science concepts in the world. They display and label each example.
  - ✓ Students take photographs of architectural elements to explain math applications in architecture. They display and label each example.

- **Fiction**

  Interested students read fiction picture books to analyze how accurately or precisely math and science concepts are incorporated. They compile an annotated bibliography of books that includes cautions regarding misinformation in the text to share with primary teachers and the librarian or media specialist. Fifth graders, for example, found an error in the binary counting sequence in the first printing of *Math Curse* by Jon Scieszka. Primary students found flawed concepts in Eric Carle's wonderful books about insects.

- **Tessellations**

  Students explore art, architecture, and design to discover math tessellations in the commercial world.

- **Glossary**
  - ✓ With collage and drawings, students develop an illustrated math glossary using practical examples of math terminology and concepts cut from newspapers, magazines, calendars, recipes, and copies of sheet music. Examples might include prime numbers, parallel lines, polygons, and sets.
  - ✓ With collage and drawings, students develop an illustrated science glossary using practical examples of science terminology and concepts cut from newspapers, magazines, moving vehicle information, cook books, and printed information or pictures from the internet. Examples might include machines, chemical changes, and forms of matter.

- **The Digital World Calendar of Math and Science**

  Students research significant accomplishments or events in math and science and plot them on a calendar. The challenge is to determine how many historical and contemporary dates they can compile on a computer calendar and then analyze patterns among these events.

- **Probability**
  As students play card games and board games, they analyze applications of probability.

- **Forensic Scientist**
  Interested students investigate to differentiate the reality of forensics from its depiction on television. Students determine what forensic scientists do, essential questions, required skills, tools, and the vocabulary of the field. Then, they watch an episode involving forensic science on television to identify misconceptions, distortions, or fallacies.

- **Interview**
  Students conduct interviews with multiple adults in a myriad of occupations to learn if and how they use math or science in their jobs.

- **Occupations**
  Students divide a chart into two columns, write math and science as the two headings, and then research and organize under each heading the jobs or professions they find in which math or science is crucial.

- **Economics**
  ✓ Students research to determine if there is a relationship between the degree of math and science a person masters and life success or life-time financial earnings one accomplishes.
  ✓ Students calculate the cost of filling the gas tank on their family vehicle and how far that vehicle travels on a full tank. They research the cost of that tank of gas last year.
  ✓ Students use different catalogs to plan a list and compare the cost of school supplies for a perfect start in middle school or high school.

- **Sports Illustrated Book of Math and Science**
  Students work together to produce a *Sports Illustrated Book of Math and Science* in which they explore, illustrate, and explain how math and science are used in several different sports.

- **Brainy Competitions**
  To determine possible participation, interested students research competitions based upon math and science expertise, such as Continental Math League, Discovery Education 3M Young Scientist Challenge, and the U.S. Department of Energy National Science Bowl.

Kingore, B. (2011). *Tiered Learning Stations in Minutes*. Austin, TX: PA Publishing.

## *Junk Shop*

**Grade Levels: K-5**

**Tiered Factors:**

- Background knowledge and skills
- Structure or complexity of the process
- Concrete or abstract thinking

The marvelous thing about the Junk Shop is its instant appeal to students and its high adaptability to applications of essential concepts and skills involving counting, matching, classification, compare and contrast, construction, and creative problem solving. The station provides hands-on learning experiences using common recyclable items. To expedite preparation, have students collect and bring to school small-sized items of *junk* from home, such a jewelry, trinkets, hardware supplies, and scraps of wood, yarn, and fabric.

### Equipment/Material

- Junk—small sized items so storage is not a problem
- Recyclable items, buttons, collage materials, math manipulatives, art materials, construction paper scraps, old jewelry, nuts/bolts and other hardware items, unusual little things
- Masking tape

### Learning Experiences

- **Number Concepts**

  Working in pairs, each child grabs a handful of junk and predicts who has the most and least. They count to check and record the numbers on a paper folded in half labeled *Least* and *Most* at the top. Children repeat the task several times and continue recording each round.Challenge students to use the terms *greater than* and *less than* as they explain their results.

- **Math Sets**

  Children count out twenty pieces of junk and organize them in groups of ten. They build something different with each group of ten, and draw a picture of each to label and  share.

Kingore, B. (2011). *Tiered Learning Stations in Minutes.* Austin, TX: PA Publishing.

- **Math Operations**

  Students select several items to use to develop a word math problem that incorporates the math operation and skills currently being studied. Challenge students to create the most complex problem they can and write its solution.

- **Crazy Creature Construction**

  Students select exactly nine items to tape together to become a Crazy Creature. On a display card (paper folded in half or thirds so it will stand), they write a description of the creature that explains its most significant attributes and what those attributes enable it to accomplish. The term *crazy creature* is used instead of more emotion-related words like monster. This term also frees children to consider all of the resulting products as being correct because they are creatures and do not have to look like a certain animal or person. After displaying for a few days, students take apart their creatures so the junk items can be used again.

- **Creative Writing**

  Students grab one handful of junk items. They write a story that incorporates each of the items in a relevant manner. An item can appear in their story numerous times but each item must be used at least once. Encourage them to draw the item into their story to create a rebus tale.

- **Description**

  ✓ Students write a description for one item. They challenge others to identify the item from the written description.

  ✓ Students write a description of one item using as extensive and varied mathematical terminology as possible.

- **Deconstruction**

  Students access simple available tools and an appliance that can not be repaired. They fold a paper in half and write *predict* as one heading and write *observe* as the second heading. On the first half, they draw and write about what they predict will be inside. After they carefully open-up the appliance, they draw and write about what they actually observed. Ask students to summarize their conclusions.

- **Analogy**

  Students create analogies to compare two junk items.

  _____ *is like* _____ *where* _____.

  _____ *is like* _____ *when* _____.

Kingore, B. (2011). *Tiered Learning Stations in Minutes*. Austin, TX: PA Publishing.

- **Quotations**
  Students collect and post quotations about junk, such as: *One man's junk is another man's treasure.* Some students pursue ways to prove or disprove the quotation. Some students research the original source or circumstance of the quotation.

## Environmental Junk Shop

- **Recyclables**
  Classify the junk shop materials into recyclable, reusable, or not recyclable boxes.

- **Recycling or Reusable Value**
  Using the available boxes of recyclable and reusable items, students select and list the ten items that they deem to have the highest recyclable or reusable value. Challenge them to figure out ways to document their conclusions.

- **Recycling in the Community**
  Students complete an alphabetical list of recyclable items commonly found at home and school. They discuss which are most abundant and which are most recycled, and then research data to assess how well the community recycles based upon this list.

- **Simple and Complex Machines**
  Students use recyclable trash to construct and demonstrate a complex machine. Then, they explain the simple machines that are also involved.

- **Survey**
  - ✓ Students survey twenty adults and twenty peers to determine their recycling practices. They ask participants to list items they recycle in each of the following categories: *most likely to recycle, sometimes recycle, seldom recycle, never recycle.* Ask each person what factors have the greatest influence on their recycling.
  - ✓ Students create a list of the *Top 10 Reasons to Recycle.*
  - ✓ Students graph the results of the items most often recycled.
  - ✓ Students analyze what conclusions might be drawn from comparing the results by age groups.
  - ✓ Students summarize their information to submit to the editorial page of a local newspaper.
  - ✓ Students research local efforts to recycle, and consider which group or groups to contact and share the information they compiled.

Kingore, B. (2011). *Tiered Learning Stations in Minutes*. Austin, TX: PA Publishing.

# Laugh Out Loud

**Grade Levels: 1-8**

**Tiered Factors:**

- Background knowledge and skills
- Structure or complexity of the process
- Complexity of product

This station is an interactive bulletin board that invites students to read and enjoy humorous text to share with peers. Cover a bulletin board with a light-colored background. Add a border and place the caption *Laughing Out Loud* at the top of the board. Provide an assortment of books containing jokes, riddles, cartoons, and word plays at various readability levels. On the floor under the bulletin board, place a few large pillows that invite students to sit or lie on the floor and read the books.

Students research to find jokes, riddles, cartoons, and word plays that they predict their peers will find the most amusing. They use brightly colored markers to write or illustrate that humorous item graffiti-style on the bulletin board paper. Under the item, students write the bibliographic reference so others can locate the original source, find needed answers to riddles or word plays, and read more items from it.

**Equipment/Material**

- Joke, cartoon, riddle, and word play books at a wide range of readability levels
- Floor pillows

**Learning Experiences**

- **Social and Emotional Sensitivity**

  As a class, discuss classroom-appropriate humor. Point out how humor that is at someone else's expense, such as put-downs and sarcasm, can be hurtful. Discuss the differences that are portrayed in the media.

Kingore, B. (2011). *Tiered Learning Stations in Minutes*. Austin, TX: PA Publishing.

- **Opinion Poll**

  After the board is full, invite students to vote for the item they think is the funniest. A small group of students collects the posted votes and ranks the results.

- **Laugh Out Loud Two**

  If enthusiasm for the station remains high, replace the background paper and activate students' interests by having students bring in the resources they propose for the station. Substitute their resources for the original ones, and repeat the appropriate learning experiences.

- **Topic-Related Riddles**

  Students create content-related riddles to place on the board for others to figure out.

- **Comics and Cartoons**

  Visual-spatial students create original comics, cartoons, and jokes to post.

- **Laugh Out Loud Literature**

  When interest in the joke books wanes, change the station to a selection of humorous literature. Place book jackets or pictures of the book covers on the board. Students read the books, rate each on a humor continuum, and register their opinion by posting a sticky-note near the book jacket on the board.

- **Vocabulary**

  Select words for the humor continuum that encourage students to analyze the nuances of word meanings. Encourage students to propose word changes to denote the levels of humor. For example, where might *chortle* or *chuckle* be placed on the continuum?

*Idea!* As with the Graffiti Board station, use a simple mnemonic device for bibliographic references by young students or students inexperienced with reference formats. Teach them *AT-CD* which stands for *Author, Title, Company, Date*. Students reference their humorous entry by writing the AT-CD facts underneath.

Kingore, B. (2011). *Tiered Learning Stations in Minutes*. Austin, TX: PA Publishing.

# Look Alikes

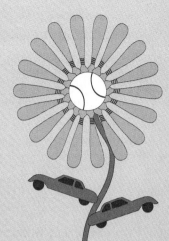

**Grade Levels: K-8**

**Tiered Factors:**

- Background knowledge and skills
- Support system
- Concrete or abstract thinking
- Complexity of product

The Look Alikes station is based upon the *Look Alikes* and *Look Alikes Jr.* books by Joan Steiner. With their clever and elaborate collage art, these books are a virtual feast for the eyes and intrigue readers to analyze details. Students typically work together searching and discussing possibilities. The initial objective of the station is to analyze each page to decipher the large number of every-day items that combine to look-like something else. When that objective is accomplished, many additional skill applications emerge. After modeling one page with the class, feature a different page each week so the center continues for a significant time.

## Equipment/Material

- *Look Alikes* and/or *Look Alikes, Jr.* by Joan Steiner
- Chart paper
- Thesaurus
- Dictionary

## Learning Experiences

- **Answer Key**
  The back of the book includes a listing of each item used on a page. To increase the students' mental engagement, tear out those pages or use self-sticking colored dots to seal together the top, sides, and bottom of the pages.

- **Matching**
  ✓ In a box lid or tray, provide several real items pictured in one photograph for young children to find and match.
  ✓ Students determine which real items to place on the tray that relate to one of the pages. They share their set as a challenge for another student.

Kingore, B. (2011). *Tiered Learning Stations in Minutes*. Austin, TX: PA Publishing.

- **Visual Discrimination**
  - ✓ Provide several items common to one photograph and challenge students to locate the correct page.
  - ✓ Provide items common to one photograph and include one item not found in that picture. Students locate the correct page and determine the item that does not belong.
  - ✓ Working in pairs, students figure out the one item that is on every page of *Look-Alikes Jr.*
  - ✓ Working in pairs, students figure out which two items can be found on every page of *Look-Alikes.*

- **Recording Written Data**

  Provide simple writing patterns that young children use to record the data from their observations. *I found sixteen crayons in the classroom picture. There are eleven tea bags on the house.*

- **Listing**

  Challenge students to make a list of all of the things found in one photograph. Invite students to compare their lists with other students to determine omitted items.

- **Alphabetizing**

  Challenge students to alphabetize their list to apply alphabetizing skills and to avoid duplications.

- **Challenge Number**

  Instead of asking students to see how many items they can find on each page, encourage a more in-depth search by posing a challenge number. A challenge number is high enough to be a challenge but low enough to be beaten. Students are more motivated to keep thinking and exert greater effort as they try to exceed the challenge number.

- **Dual Languages**

  Divide a chart paper in half and write a different language as the heading for the columns. Students list the items found in one photograph in each language.

- **Collage Art**
  - ✓ Children use small concrete items to create collage art.
  - ✓ Students use small items and cut out pictures to create a collage self-portrait.
  - ✓ Students select small items and cut out pictures that are of personal significance. After creating collage portraits or pictures of themselves and their family, they write to explain how each item is significant to them.

Kingore, B. (2011). *Tiered Learning Stations in Minutes*. Austin, TX: PA Publishing.

✓ After creating collage self-portraits using personally significant items, students write several similes or metaphors to explain how they are like the items. *I love jelly beans and my Grandma thinks I am as sweet as my jelly bean teeth.*

✓ To demonstrate their comprehension of a significant character, students select cut out pictures and small items to create look-alike collages that represent the traits of that character. They write an explanation of their collages.

✓ Students use small items and cut out pictures to create look-alike collages.

 ***Caution!*** Look-alike collages are more difficult than they seem and may frustrate some students.

- **Descriptive Writing**

✓ Students revisit their list of items in a picture and use a thesaurus to search for rich descriptive words to each item to increase its appeal. For example, *tea bags* was embellished to *bags of cinnamon apple green tea.*

✓ Students revisit their lists with descriptive phrases, select three to five of the phrases to incorporate into a descriptive paragraph, and post their paragraphs to share with the class. Children read each others' and try to match the title for the picture to the paragraph.

✓ Challenge students to use alliterative phrases to describe an item, such as *an amazing amusement park.*

✓ To increase the challenge, students write alliterative sentences to describe and explain an item, such as *The art of an amazing American amusement park ambitiously amasses a number of ambiguous items.*

- **Digital Photographs**

Students use a digital camera to photograph items in the real world that look like something else, such as a rock that resembles a face.

- **Math**

✓ Number
  - Young children count the number of items on a page.
  - Children count the number of *different* items on a page and compare that number with the total number of items.

Kingore, B. (2011). *Tiered Learning Stations in Minutes.* Austin, TX: PA Publishing.

✓ Comparative Thinking
  – Children use greater than and less than symbols to discuss and compare quantities of the items.
✓ Fractions, Percentages, and Ratios
  – Students develop statements expressing the quantities of items as fractions, percentages, or ratios.
✓ Word Problems
  – Students refer to the items in one photograph and write word problems using that data. Specify the kind of problem students are to develop so the problems will demonstrate students' comprehension of current math concepts.

• **Elaboration**

To emphasize the value of detail and elaboration, students compare a picture from *Look Alikes, Jr.* with a picture from *Look Alikes.* Since *Look Alikes, Jr.* uses over 700 common objects and *Look Alikes* draws from 1000 or more common objects, the detail in *Look Alikes* is greater and often more complex. Challenge students to write a paragraph about themselves that uses some appropriate detail and description and then construct a second version of the same paragraph that embellishes the original version with more extensive, complex information and description.

• **Analogies**

After multiple experiences with the book, students select one item on a page and develop three or more analogies comparing how that item is similar to what it is pretending to be. (Requiring multiple analogies increases the depth of thinking.)

> *The dog biscuits are like the bricks on a chimney because:*
> 1. *Their shape lets them fit together.*
> 2. *They are produced in different colors and textures.*
> 3  *They are solids.*
> 4. *They are related to survival. Dogs need food to survive and people need shelters to survive.*
> 5. *They are man-made.*

• **Evaluation and Ranking**

Students review and rank their multiple analogies. They conclude by writing an explanation of which criteria they used to determine their rankings.

Kingore, B. (2011). *Tiered Learning Stations in Minutes.* Austin, TX: PA Publishing.

# Mathematical Explorations

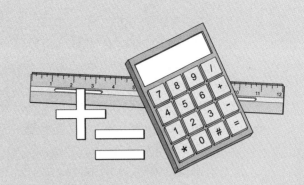

**Grade Levels: K-8**

**Tiered Factors:**

- Background knowledge and skills
- Support system
- Structure or complexity of the process
- Resources

This station incorporates open-ended activities and hands-on materials for applications and practice experiences related to current math concepts and skills. The learning experiences encourage students to explore relationships, approach math tasks in various ways at differing levels of complexity, and organize data as well as compute a solution.

## Equipment/Material

- Math problems tiered by complexity
- Math manipulatives and tools
- Graph paper
- Math picture books
- List of websites with math games and challenges at different levels of complexity

## Learning Experiences

- **Computer Applications**
  - ✓ According to assessed needs, students use computer programs for grade-level math applications or to develop advanced math skills and concepts.
  - ✓ Post a short list of approved websites with math connections. Individual students elect to explore one or more of the sites.

- **Demonstrations**
  - ✓ In pairs, students select from tiered math problems to prepare a three-to-five minute demonstration that explains the problem to classmates. Encourage students to incorporate illustrations, graphs, and manipulatives as appropriate. Provide time in class for students to model their demonstrations in small groups.
  - ✓ As another authentic audience, arrange for students to meet with the teacher of a

Kingore, B. (2011). *Tiered Learning Stations in Minutes*. Austin, TX: PA Publishing.

younger class and agree upon a math problem appropriate for that age group. Students then plan how to teach to a small group of younger children using diagrams, manipulatives, and interaction.

✓ Individually or in pairs, students select from a provided list of concepts and prepare diagrams to demonstrate that concept to small groups of classmates. Students select from concepts such as the following or propose a different concept to illustrate.
  – Linear sequence of time
  – Mean, median, and mode
  – Relationship of fractions to percents
  – Proving the Pythagorean theorem

- **Three Ways**

  Individually or in pairs, students select a tiered math problem from current study and then write and illustrate three ways to solve the problem.

- **Paper Chains**

  Assign students numbers either randomly or based upon their readiness. Using provided paper cut into strips, students create a math chain for a designated number. On the first link of the chain, students list their assigned numeral and number word. Each link added to to the chain lists an equation that would result in that number. Challenge students to construct a long chain that incorporates as many operations skills, and steps as they are able to demonstrate.

- **Creating Math Word Problems**

  To demonstrate mastery, students write, illustrate, and complete their own examples of math word problems using the skills and concepts currently being studied.

- **Matching Game**

  Students write math word problems on several different cards and illustrate them on separate cards. Peers put the problem and illustration back together as a matching task.

- **Graphs**

  Students research math questions of personal interest to collect data relating to current topics of study. They create and post original graphs to illustrate the relationships they conclude. For example, these questions emerged during a study of Africa. How has the total number of these seven endangered animals changed over a 30 year period? What are the most prevalent occupations of adults in Africa compared to the United States?

Kingore, B. (2011). *Tiered Learning Stations in Minutes*. Austin, TX: PA Publishing.

- **Tangrams**
  - ✓ Provide cardstock templates for the tangram. Students copy and cut out their own sets of the seven tans and write their initials in each to identify which side is up. They create animals and other figures using all seven tans in such a way that they touch but do not overlap. Students glue a completed tangram figure on an index card, autograph it, and post it to share with others.
  - ✓ Students challenge themselves to work together to produce the numerals 0-9 using the seven tans to create each numeral. Glue the completed numerals on index cards to display.
  - ✓ Challenge students to work together to produce the alphabet using the seven tans to create each letter. Glue the completed alphabet letters on index cards to display.
  - ✓ Students write directions so that someone is able to duplicate a completed tangram figure without seeing the original.

- **Math Literature**

  After reading readiness-appropriate math picture books, students write and illustrate their own books incorporating specific math terminology and concepts. The following is a brief sample of books that work particularly well for this learning experience.
  - *Ten Black Dots* by Donald Crew (number sense)
  - *The Best of Times* by Greg Tang (multiplication)
  - *If You Hopped Like a Frog* by David Schwartz (ratio)
  - *Sir Cumference and the Sword in the Cone* by Cindy Neuschwander (geometric solids)
  - *Skittles Riddles* by Barbiere McGrath (equations and fractions)
  - *Alexander, Who Used to Be Rich Last Sunday* by Judith Viorst (money and sequence)

- **Math Process Letters**

  To demonstrate mastery, students write a letter to a real or fictitious person of their choice to explain how to work a math problem that represents the skills and concepts currently being studied.

- **Math Autobiography**

  Students write their math autobiography by incorporating as many numbers as possible that are relevant to their life. If interested, students read *Math Curse* by Jon Scieszka as a model.

Kingore, B. (2011). *Tiered Learning Stations in Minutes*. Austin, TX: PA Publishing.

# Reading Retreat

**Grade Levels: K-8**

**Tiered Factors:**

- Background knowledge and skills
- Support system
- Concrete or abstract thinking
- Resources

The Reading Retreat is a station that enables students to spend significant blocks of time engaged in reading independently and listening to language. The station is easily adjusted to diverse reading abilities and interests by offering a wide range of quality literature at different reading levels to insure that students have the opportunity to read at their highest level of comprehension. The power to choose reading topics and materials increases students' ownership and motivation to excel.

## Equipment/Material

✎ A range of quality literature and comic books, both fiction and nonfiction

✎ Recording device and recorded books for students to listen to and follow along

✎ Music CDs and earphones for students to listen to music as they read

✎ Students' published stories, nonfiction articles, and class books

✎ Pillows that invite stretching out and enjoying a great book

## Learning Experiences

- **Interest Survey**

  Students complete and post inter-est surveys regarding what they like to read and want to learn more about. The survey can be written statements or, particularly for young and special needs students, drawings and words to represent their interests. Ask students to vary the size of their drawings to denote the intensity of that interest. Posting the surveys decorates the station and provides ways for students to learn about others who share their interests. Work with the school library and or media specialist to bring materials into the station in response to students' interests.

- **Read Along**
  - ✓ Provide recordings of class-experienced books for students to elect to listen to again for language support and enjoyment.
  - ✓ Students create recordings of favorite literature for others to listen and read-along.

- **Student Publications**

  Feature class-written books and student published works at the station to insure a class-wide audience for their stories, poems, and articles.

- **Rating System**

  Students develop a rating system for books and post their ratings to share their perspectives and opinions with classmates. Students are interested in books highly rated by peers.

- **Literature Mural**

  Tape a long piece of light colored butcher paper on the wall of the station at children's eye level. Over time, students complete a collaborative mural by adding an illustration representing their favorite books or characters.

- **Comic Books**

  Provide comic books that are appropriate in tone and content for the age of the students. Comic books have a surprisingly complex vocabulary level. Krashen's *The Power of Reading* lists reading levels of 4.4 to 6.4 for comic books with Spiderman or Batman.

- **Literary Puzzlers**

  Each day, feature a different quotation or line from a book and challenge students to figure out the book's title and author. Students post their answer under the quotation. With experience, challenge students to produce literary puzzlers for peers to decipher.

- **Literary Reviews**

  Students write and post reviews of available books. Encourage them to submit their reviews for posting throughout the school or publishing on internet sources.

- **Thematic Literature**

  Provide a collection of books that relate to the same theme. Students select which ones they want to read and reflect upon the book's application of that theme.

Kingore, B. (2011). *Tiered Learning Stations in Minutes*. Austin, TX: PA Publishing.

# *Sketch Artists*

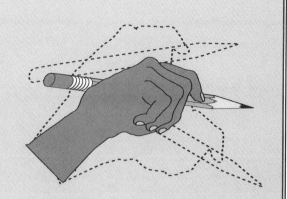

**Grade Levels: K-8**

**Tiered Factors:**

- Background knowledge and skills
- Structure or complexity of the process
- Concrete or abstract thinking
- Complexity of product

This station honors visual-spatial and bodily-kinesthetic learners as it involves all students in art connections to content. Some students decide they are not good at art. The intent of this station is to foster creative responses and adaptations for all students through simple prompts and tasks that encourage students that they do not need  sophisticated art techniques in order to draw. The learning experiences emphasize simple, less-messy art tasks that student complete independently.

Research documents that art responses provide students additional contexts to augment memory and comprehension—particularly regarding specific subject vocabulary (ASCD, 2006). These station tasks focus on active engagement and personal interpretation of content. Use  the term *quick sketch* to infer that a representation rather than a finely developed illustration is the goal. Sketching activates right-brain responses to content by asking students to graphically represent information.

**Equipment/Material**

- Extensive variety of drawing materials and colors
- Diverse mediums such as water colors, Cray-Pas™, charcoal, and chalk
- Sketch paper or newsprint pads
- Computer resources for clip art
- Free-standing photograph frames

**Learning Experiences**

- **Math Word Problems**
  Students illustrate a math word problem.

Kingore, B. (2011). *Tiered Learning Stations in Minutes*. Austin, TX: PA Publishing.

- **Interests**

  Students quick-sketch a collage of their favorite things and autograph their pictures to display at a gallery of students' interests. Provide picture frames in which students place their work for a more finished and prestigious gallery.

- **Shaped Paper**

  Provide large paper cut in one or more shapes related to a current topic, such as an historical monument, a polygon, or a specific species of animal. Students quick-sketch related words and images graffiti-style inside the shape.

- **Mural**

  Provide a large piece of butcher paper along one wall at students' eye level. Students collaboratively work over time to develop a mural that relates to the current topic of study, such as oceanography.

- **Transformation**

  Provide the book *The Dot* by Peter Reynolds. Children draw a dot on their paper in one bright color. Then, they use contrasting colors to elaborate and illustrate what that dot can become. Display the finished works under the following caption.

  *I was a dot, but now I am* _____.

- **Primary-Secondary Colors**
  - ✓ After mixing food coloring with water to create primary colors in small plastic tumblers, students use eye droppers to extract a small amount of one primary color and release two separate drops of color onto water-color paper or a coffee-filter paper. They then select a second primary color to add to the second drop of the first color. On writing paper, using colored markers or map pens to replicate the colors on their report, they record the sequence of their process and the color that results, such as *red + blue = purple*. Students then draw a line sketch of an item or figure of their choice using the created color. Students repeat the process using other color combinations, recording their results, and sketching in that color.
  - ✓ Students expand the primary-secondary color experience to create a rainbow or a complete color wheel.

- **Computer Clip Art**

  Students select a piece of clip art related to a class topic of study and then sketch a scene or related details to embellish the original drawing.

Kingore, B. (2011). *Tiered Learning Stations in Minutes*. Austin, TX: PA Publishing.

- **Rebus Writing**

  Students sketch multiple small pictures to substitute for nouns, adjectives, and verbs in a sentence, paragraph, story, math problem or lab report they are writing. Young students can use thumbprint drawings for their rebus pictures.

- **Alphabet Book**

  Students create an alphabet book by illustrating each letter and transforming it into an object that begins with the sound of that letter. Provide this writing template for students who would benefit from this support. *This use to be an A. Now it is an antelope.* As appropriate, challenge students to avoid common letter-sound connections such as *A* and *apple.*

- **Task Cards**

  Provide task cards with tiered tasks that students sketch on a paper to demonstrate their comprehension of math, science, and social studies terminology. The tasks can be as simple or complex as appropriate to students' readiness. Several examples follow to prompt thinking.

  – *Draw three black rectangles.*
  – *Draw a set of four little yellow circles inside a large blue oval.*
  – *Sketch an insect and list six attributes it illustrates that are applicable to real insects.*
  – *Sketch the globe and draw dark lines identifying the equator and the Tropic of Cancer.*
  – *Draw a hexagon inside an octagon.*
  – *Draw a polygon whose number of angles is a prime number.*
  – *Draw an acute angle and an obtuse angle between parallel lines.*
  – *Sketch a microscope and label four key features that enable the microscope to work effectively.*
  – *Sketch a map of Africa and include as many countries as you can. Then, study a map of Africa and return to use a second color to embellish or correct your first sketch.*

- **Symmetry**

  Provide one-half of a simple picture or clip art. Students glue the picture on a paper and sketch the missing half of the picture so the picture is complete again.

- **Literature Connections**

  Rather than simply draw a picture of a story or character, students enjoy the benefit of the art connection while using more academic skills. Develop task cards that integrate higher

Kingore, B. (2011). *Tiered Learning Stations in Minutes*. Austin, TX: PA Publishing.

skill connections, such as the following examples.

- *Draw a picture of the protagonist the first time he or she appears in the story.*
- *Sketch a sequence showing the five most important events in order in the story.*
- *Sketch three objects that are crucial in the story. Explain why each is significant.*
- *Sketch the turning point of the story.*
- *Create symbols to represent the traits of each key character.*

- **Comics**

Students draw comic strips or cartoons to explain classroom topics, summarize a story, or delineate the sequence of a process in math, science, or social studies.

- **Word Visualizations**

Students create word visualizations by artistically writing the word in a way to denote its meaning.

**thick**      *funny*      *elaborate*

- **Vocabulary**

Working in pairs, one student begins a quick sketch that denotes a content-specific word while the other student watches and tries to identify the picture, state the vocabulary word, and spell it as the sketch is completed.

- **Abstract Thinking**

Students draw symbols to represent a concept or summarize a story They include three to five clues for others to use to decipher the symbols. If preferred, students add a paper flap for others to lift to reveal the answer.

Kingore, B. (2011). *Tiered Learning Stations in Minutes*. Austin, TX: PA Publishing.

## *Tech Apps*

**Grade Levels: K-8**

**Tiered Factors:**

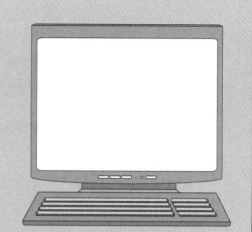

- Background knowledge and skills
- Support system
- Structure or complexity of the process
- Concrete or abstract thinking
- Resources
- Complexity of product

Students of all ages love technology, are fluent in applying it, and are motivated by its many diverse applications. The objective of this station is to provide authentic applications, or tech apps, of technology across the curriculum to foster students' continued learning of essential concepts and skills. Research documents that computer applications increase achievement, particularly in vocabulary development and math skills (Marzano, 2004; Wolfe, 2001).

**Equipment/Material**

- Computers and applicable software programs
- Auditory recording equipment
- Digital camera
- List of websites with academic connections

**Learning Experiences**

- **Software Applications**

  Students are assigned or select software applications to practice and extend essential skills and concepts. The applications provide varied levels to insure that students at all levels of readiness experience continuous learning.

- **Beginning Tech Apps**
  - ✓ Word processor

    Students who consider themselves to be writers use the computer to create fiction or nonfiction works before publishing their compositions. Encourage them to seek assistance from the Editor's Office learning station.

✓ Illustrations
Students use the draw features of the computer to add visual interest to their products and PowerPoint™ slides with illustrations, borders, clip art, and symbolic representations.
✓ Photography
Student photographers process and print their photographs. Others use software programs such as Photoshop™ to edit and revise photographs.

• **Digital Portfolio**
Students develop and update personal products in a digital portfolio to document their achievements and change over time as learners. Students also store lists of favorite books read and to be read.

• **Class Portfolio**
A digital class portfolio is an appealing component to reflect the achievements and projects of the class as a whole. Typically, weekly entries are made to herald the content and experiences of the class. Students take turns serving as the class historian who makes choices about what to record and which examples to scan and include as a representative sample of the learning topics, skills, and events of that week in class. Eventually, every student should have the opportunity to serve as class historian. The class portfolio becomes a collective scrapbook or data base representing the curriculum and class experiences for the entire year. It is a unique opportunity for students to select work and reflect upon learning accomplishments as a community of learners rather than only as individuals.

• **Class Blog**
One or more students work together to create a class blog. Classmates make daily additions to the blog to maintain a community journal of their reflections. Students post creative writing and essays on the blog to insure an audience for their work.

• **Class Newspaper**
Using a newspaper software program, students work together to produce a bi-weekly or monthly newspaper for the class. Students design the logos and layout of the paper. Some students specialize as reporters, editors, or photographers. Students elect to or take turns serving as the editor responsible for the final printing.

• **Read Along**
Students produce read-along recordings for younger students to use. They begin by interviewing a teacher of a younger grade level to determine which library books would benefit

and interest the young children. Next, one or more students produce the recording and incorporate character voices, simple sound effects, and a signal for when to turn the page. The recording and a copy of the book are then delivered to the younger classroom for those students to enjoy.

- **Digit-Cam Lab**

  Students sign up as instructors in the Digit-Cam Lab. In the lab, students work with students to teach them how to be more effective and creative with digital photography. They also share points and procedures for developing dynamic PowerPoint™ presentations using their pictures. Additionally, some students specialize in teaching how to use voice-over narration and insert music.

- **Websites**

  ✓ Post a short list of approved websites with academic connections. Individual students elect to explore and experience one or more of the sites.

  ✓ Invite students to propose additional sites they find that offer appropriate skill applications. To propose a site, a student writes a proposal explaining the academic value of the site and includes reasons why classmates will benefit from the site. A class committee and the teacher review the proposal and research the site before it is added to the recommended list.

 *Caution!* Promote internet credibility. Invite a technology specialist to talk with the class regarding how to critique Internet sources for their value, credibility, and accuracy. Involve students in critically evaluating fraudulent and scam web sites, and discuss what students find suspicious about those sites. Students are more sophisticated consumers when armed with critical evaluation tools.

- **Evaluation Graph**

  Post a large graph with the recommended academic websites as the column headings. List the name of each student as a row heading. When a student uses one of the websites, that student rates the value of the experience on a continuum of one to five, with one being low and five being a highly worthwhile website. Encourage students to discuss or question the ratings with peers. Over time, use the results to determine which sites to continue to recommend. Students are often interested in and influenced by peer evaluations.

- **Photograph–Compare and Contrast**

  Students use a digital camera to take one photograph. Before they view it, they draw and

Kingore, B. (2011). *Tiered Learning Stations in Minutes*. Austin, TX: PA Publishing.

color a sketch of what they think the photo will show. Then, they compare their drawing with the photograph and write two or three ways the two are similar and different.

- **School Scenes**
  ✓ Students take digital pictures of school scenes or people working at school. Using the word processor, they write a clear, detailed description of the contents of the photograph and then load the picture on the computer.
  ✓ After several description and photograph entries, School Scenes becomes a thinking task for others to use. Classmates read a description and draw the scene they visualize before comparing their drawing with the original photograph.

- **Web Masters**
  Students sign up as web masters to help others create their own websites.

- **Time to Reflect: The Good, the Bad, and the Ugly**
  The role and value of technology in our global world is an issue that merits consideration. In preparation, ask students to reflect and jot down notes regarding their views. Ask them to evaluate the topic in terms of its current status and future trends. Later, have students conduct a discussion in which they share their reflections and organize their consensus into the good, the bad, and the ugly about the current and future state of technology in our society.

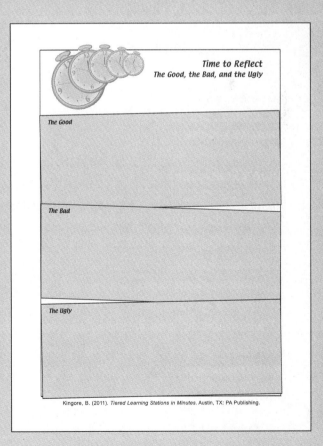

*Time to Reflect*
The Good, the Bad, and the Ugly

The Good

The Bad

The Ugly

Kingore, B. (2011). *Tiered Learning Stations in Minutes*. Austin, TX: PA Publishing.

Kingore, B. (2011). *Tiered Learning Stations in Minutes*. Austin, TX: PA Publishing.

# *Think Tank*

**Grade Levels: 3-8**

**Tiered Factors:**

- Background knowledge and skills
- Support system
- Structure or complexity of the process
- Concrete or abstract thinking

This station is developed around high-interest logic problems that entice students to read, write, and think as they explore logic problems and creative thinking across curriculum areas. The intent is to mentally engage students in high-level thinking and content-related essential skills and concepts rather than for them to simply experience logic tasks. Access logic problems from resources in the library or online and select those that are classroom-relevant.

## Equipment/Material

 Index cards

 Logic problems with skill and content connections

## Learning Experiences

- **Logic Problems**

  On cards, provide a set of six to eight logic tasks that use classroom significant skills or concepts, such as the examples here that require students to figure out the missing operations in math problems or replace icons with letters to identify related science concepts. After developing several task cards, tier the problems so some entail more simple, concrete thinking and others require complex, abstract thinking. Each student selects one logic task card and works to find the solution(s).

  $$8 \; ? \; 7 \; ? \; 2 \; ? \; 4 \; ? \; 5 = 20 \qquad \ast \; \square \; a \; \blacklozenge \; \ast \; t \; \vert$$

- **Support**

  Encourage students who have less experience with logic tasks to work with a peer at the station.

Kingore, B. (2011). *Tiered Learning Stations in Minutes*. Austin, TX: PA Publishing.

- **Student Checker**

  On a rotating basis, designate one student as the checker. When students complete a logic problem, they record the solution in their station log and take their log to the student checker who has the answer key. The checker is only allowed to confirm that the student's task is complete or tell the student to revisit the problem.

- **Strategist**

  Rather than share the solution when they successfully decipher one of the logic problems, students explain and use nonpermanent adhesive to post the strategy they used. They either write what worked for them or which strategy they tried that was not productive. At no point do they reveal their solution to other students who might later work on the same logic task. Students benefit from analyzing strategies.

- **Students as Producers**

  After successful experiences with the Think Tank station, change the objective. Now, when students come to this station, they select a card to use as an example. Rather than complete the logic card task, students create a new task card using the selected card as an example. When complete, they post their new card. The next person arriving at the station must work the student-produced logic problem before selecting a different card they use to produce another original example. When students become producers, they operate at high levels of thinking as they analyze and synthesize.

- **Self-Perpetuating Station**

  This station now perpetuates itself without significant teacher intervention. Adults facilitate skill and concept integration by the kinds of content-connected logic problems they provide at the station as models for the students. Students continue to produce different logic problems for other students to complete.

 *Idea!* A resource of logic problems created by Mensa, the high IQ society, is particularly applicable to this station. Sets of logic tasks using content skills and concepts are organized into decks of seventy-five cards each. There are two levels: *Genius Decks* and *Genius Deck for Kids*. The first level fosters high-level thinking for grade six through adult; the second level is effective with grades one through five. The seventy-five cards in each set are ample for a year-long station.

Kingore, B. (2011). *Tiered Learning Stations in Minutes*. Austin, TX: PA Publishing.

# *Travel Planner*

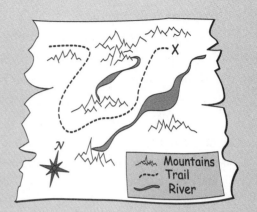

**Grade Levels: 2-8**

**Tiered Factors:**

- Background knowledge and skills
- Support system
- Structure or complexity of the process
- Concrete or abstract thinking
- Resources
- Complexity of product

This station uses open-ended activities that incorporate social studies, reading, writing, and high-level thinking to learn about our world. It fosters high-interest participation as most students are fascinated with travel. The learning experiences encourage students to approach tasks in various ways and at differing levels of complexity as they explore relationships and organize data.

## Equipment/Material

- Magazines in a wide variety of readability levels, such as travel magazines and *National Geographic*
- Nonfiction resources
- Internet access
- Pictures of famous locations
- Travel brochures

## Learning Experiences

- **Favorite Places**
  - ✓ Invite students to post pictures, a description, and why they like a favorite place. The site can be their home, a popular local park, a zoo, or a far-off location.
  - ✓ If appropriate to the background experiences of the students, post a United States or world map to highlight the places students have traveled or lived. Students use a push pin to designate a location they experienced and extend a piece of yarn from that push pin to a four-by-six inch index card on which they write about their experiences at that location.

Kingore, B. (2011). *Tiered Learning Stations in Minutes*. Austin, TX: PA Publishing.

- **Flap Book of Travels**

  Children read Rod Campbell's *Dear Zoo* about a child writing to the zoo for a pet. Use the repeating template: *I went to_____to find me_____. It was too_____.* Students create an interactive travel book that incorporates the flora, fauna, and topography of a country or location. They write about one example on each page and cover the illustration with a flap to cause the reader to predict.

  > *I went to the Sahara Desert to find me a camel. It was too mean and spit at me.*

  > *I went to the Sahara Desert to find me a sand dune. It was too shifty.*

- **Travel Choices**

  ✓ Students research places they are interested in visiting. They draw pictures and explain why they want to visit that place.

  ✓ Students compute and compare the cost of traveling to their chosen location by at least two different modes of transportation, such as taking a cruise versus flying and driving.

  ✓ *Where am I?* Students write and illustrate riddles that share several attributes of an area or location and challenge others to figure out the place they want to visit.

  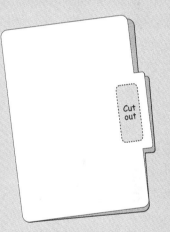

  ✓ *Coordinate Riddles.* Students write and illustrate riddles that provide the latitude and longitude of a site and challenge others to figure out the location they want to visit.

  ✓ Students draw maps with a legend that includes as extensive detail as possible about the area and the most important sites to experience.

- **Featured Country or Area**

  ✓ Fill the station with multiple resources, pictures, and posters about a specific location or geographic area, such as a city or country the class is studying.

  ✓ Students cut a file folder to resemble a suitcase. After learning about the area, they write on the outside of the folder-suitcase where they are going, their travel plan, and agenda. Inside the folder-suitcase, they glue cut outs of the kinds of items that they would need to pack in order to visit and enjoy that location, such as kinds of clothing, shoes, and sun screen.

  ✓ Students work alone or with another student to complete a list of significant information about the area organized for every letter of the alphabet.

  ✓ Students research and graph the weather for the area and explain how it affects population patterns and lifestyles.

Kingore, B. (2011). *Tiered Learning Stations in Minutes.* Austin, TX: PA Publishing.

✓ Students research customs for the area and, if the language is not English, learn key phrases to teach others.

✓ Students develop a travel brochure or sales presentation with information and illustrations that entice others to visit and spend more tourist dollars in their economy.

- **It's a Mystery**

  Post a picture of a famous monument, building, attraction, or location with the caption: *Where am I and what is my name?* Challenge students to figure out the mystery. Add a clue each day until someone deciphers the challenge.

- **Survival**

  Students create an illustrated, informative guide about what to do, what to bring, and how to survive when traveling in a specific harsh environment, such as a desert or swamp.

- **Expert**

  Students select a country, continent, region, or city that fascinates them enough that they want to develop expertise in that site. After research and interviews, students develop an interactive lesson to teach others about the site by developing a PowerPoint™, demonstration, game, video, or theatrical play. They can also elect to role play the president of the Chamber of Commerce and be prepared to respond to any question others pose about the area. Additionally, they prepare a list of appropriate resources students can access to acquire free maps, posters, and information and create a rubric or evaluation tool that others use to assess the lesson.

- **Travel Trunk Puzzler**

  Students work together to create a travel trunk puzzler out of a shoe box. The intent is to represent a location with artifacts so others have to figure out the site. As a class, agree upon the kinds of information every travel trunk puzzler must include, such as data about the people, geography, government, lifestyle, ceremonies, customs, and economy. Inside the box, students place symbols, words, complete and incomplete pictures, part of a drawn map, and other information as clues for others to decipher. Students decorate their travel trunk before making it available to classmates or another class to analyze.

Kingore, B. (2011). *Tiered Learning Stations in Minutes*. Austin, TX: PA Publishing.

## *TWELVE STATION IDEAS ESPECIALLY FOR YOUNG LEARNERS*

The descriptions that follow are ideas for additional high-interest, low-preparation learning stations with particular applications for young learners. These stations readily integrate discovery, kinesthetic experiences, and curriculum priorities in primary classrooms, such as the development of vocabulary, writing, and reading skills. Simultaneously, the learning experience in these stations invite children to practice the social skills that adults value for young learners. These stations incorporate significant learning experiences that can be accomplished by students with entry-level, academic skills.

As frequently as possible in each station, model specific, higher-level vocabulary related to the learning tasks. For example, as children use a screw driver in the Construction Zone, use the terms *clockwise* and *counterclockwise*. In the Animals Read and Listen Place and in the Write On stations, encourage children to incorporate terminology such as *author, illustrator, antagonist* and *protagonist* as they work together. Children learn well the language adults use consistently in authentic contexts.

### Acting Theater

At the Acting Theater, children explore by role playing scenes from daily life, such as in a home, doctor's office, store, restaurant, post office, or bank. To pique children's imagination, supply simple props, such as a towel for a bed, small shelves, a box for a table or desk, menus, and catalogs. At another time, set up the Acting Theater so children role play scenarios between characters in the stories the class is reading.

As a further variation, children can practice and perform choral reading and readers theater scripts at this station. Forge connections between home and school by encouraging children to discuss prop ideas with parents and siblings at home and plan appropriate items to incorporate in the station. As frequently as possible, provide opportunities for children to perform their creative dramatics for others in the class, in another class, or for visitors in the class.

### The Animals Read and Listen Place

Place a collection of stuffed animals atop a book shelf filled with quality fiction and nonfiction books. Children select an animal to read a story to or an animal to hold as they listen to a recorded story and read along in the book.

---

Kingore, B. (2011). *Tiered Learning Stations in Minutes.* Austin, TX: PA Publishing.

Picture books about animals are a natural component at this station, but also supply class-made books, wordless books, and class favorites as part of the reading selections. Provide an abundant selection of nonfiction books about topics that reflect children's interests. Children are eager to read about their topics of interest and research supports that they develop a higher vocabulary when reading materials about their specific interests. Include recording devices so interested children can record a story as a read-along for others.

## Construction Zone

This hands-on station includes a variety of manipulatives such as blocks, Legos™, straws, and Play Dough™ for building and problem solving. Enhance the learning potential by having children write how-to sequences or draw plans for construc-

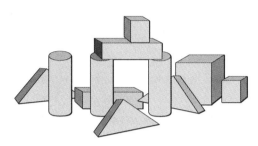

tion projects before they begin or after completion of the tasks. Some children enjoy using a variety of software that allows the manipulation of graphics to develop construction plans. Post the plans that children develop for others to follow to complete a construction when working at the station. Children can also draw the outline of a single-layer block construction, label with the number of blocks used, and challenge others to use the same number of blocks to re-create the structure from the drawing.

### Nifty Numbers

This hands-on station provides a variety of manipulatives to engage children in tasks involving number sense. Graphs, clocks, dice, magnetic numerals, Sudoku puzzles, phone key pads, and counters engage students in mathematical challenges. Students incorporate the manipulatives into pictorial math word problems and equations that practice and extend math skills and vocabulary. Students complete provided learning experiences or develop challenges for others.

## Portfolio Station

This station includes all of the materials, forms, and hanging files students need to organize products for

Kingore, B. (2011). *Tiered Learning Stations in Minutes*. Austin, TX: PA Publishing.

their portfolios. It provides the place and appropriate time for children to complete their learning reflections and select the portfolio entries that herald their learning. A chart in the station is a useful communication tool to remind beginning readers of the process for completing a portfolio entry.

### Projection

The overhead or document camera in this station invites children to use an overhead transparency or a paper on the document pad to practice writing numerals, the alphabet, words, and sentences. They also complete other fine-motor tasks such as drawing polygons or pictures. Then, students project their work onto a chalkboard or whiteboard and use their large muscles to trace the letters, words, and illustrations they produced.

As a skill and content extension, provide transparencies or papers with topic information presented in a cloze format--key words in the text replaced with a blank. Children practice comprehension skills as they write the missing words in each blank and then project the results to trace on the chalkboard or whiteboard.

### Scientific Discoveries

This hands-on station involves all of the senses in scientific explorations. The equipment and problem-solving tasks provide budding scientists with multiple opportunities to observe, predict, compare, illustrate, record, and write. The station contains plants, rocks, fossils, bones, magnifying glasses, an aquarium or class pet, tiered learning tasks, and several books with related information and illustrations. The learning tasks are planned to use the skills of observation, compare and contrast, inference, and writing words and sentences.

### Sounds of Music

Children celebrate the joy of music and experiment with sound by experiencing a range of musical instruments provided at the station. Brief and simple musical scores encourage children to read the music and play along. Provide instructions for making simple musical instruments. Children can follow the directions and create their own instruments to use to accompany recorded music.

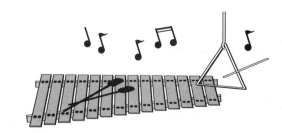

Kingore, B. (2011). *Tiered Learning Stations in Minutes*. Austin, TX: PA Publishing.

To encourage students to be composers, feature books of simple, well-known songs and provide audio recorders and staff paper for writing music.

Supply simple instrumental recordings of well-known children's songs, such as *Ring Around the Rosie* and *The Farmer in the Dell*. Encourage children to write different lyrics to sing to these tunes and then record their versions or provide opportunities for them to perform for others. Invite children to write songs incorporating information relating to current topics of study

### Thinking About Me (or Thinking About Us)

This station promotes a celebration of individuals or the entire class. Children draw and post self-portraits or drawings of classmates involved in classroom scenes. Provide a digital camera and invite children to photograph and post pictures with captions and explanations about themselves,

friends, and family. Include a rich array of books with stories that celebrate being a child.

Children can complete interest surveys, lists of their favorite things, informative graphs that compare their preferences, family trees, and drawings that illustrate what is important to them. They also write stories and riddles about individual or class experiences for others to read or decipher.

A learning experience popular with primary children and their families is to have the children create alphabet books about themselves. Each child writes, illustrates, and organizes important things about her or him for every letter of the alphabet. Extend the task by inviting the children to be alliterative and include with each letter as many words as they can weave in that also begin with the sound of that letter.

### Wonderful Words

Inasmuch as vocabulary development is integral to comprehension and learning to read, this station offers experiences that engage children in learning and using wonderful words. Intriguing challenges with letters and words invite children to play a variety of games and word puzzles. Reference materials, and manipulatives, such as magnetic letters, are included to encourage children to practice and extend their vocabulary and language arts skills.

Provide books that celebrate vocabulary and interesting words, such as *Dear Deer: A Book of Homophones* by Gene Barretta, *Some Smug Slug* by Pamela Edwards, and *Thesaurus Rex* by Laya

---

Kingore, B. (2011). *Tiered Learning Stations in Minutes*. Austin, TX: PA Publishing.

Steinberg. *The Boy Who Loved Words* by Roni Schotter motivates children to cut words out of magazines, newspapers, and advertisements to make a collection of words they love. Prepare a class bulletin board where children illustrate and post words that they love, such as *humongous* written extremely large and bold.

## A World of People

Children explore nonfiction print and internet resources to investigate social studies connections involving maps, cultures, and the daily life of people in the past, present, and future. Include an abundance of richly-illustrated literature related to different cultures and locations. Provide a mirror, simple props, and costumes that invite children to dress up as people from different times and places as they interact and dialogue with peers. Encourage children to prepare oral presentations and simple props to teach others what they learn about this world of people.

If children of diverse cultures are in the class, feature photographs and materials from their culture and arrange ways for them to teach the other children about their culture. If multi-lingual children are in the class, have children interview them and ask them to help the class learn several important words in their first language to the class.

## Write On!

Entice children to be authors by displaying an interesting variety of writing tools, colored paper, unexpected items that promote descriptions, a pictorial directory with children's names and addresses, and varied sources of print. Children complete individual stories, reports about topics of interest, and entries in class books.

Over time, invite students to collaboratively develop and post an extensive list of authentic reasons to write so children come to understand that writing is communication with daily applications.

If it is possible to locate the writing station near a bulletin board or large poster, divide the board into boxes labeled alphabetically. Children write illustrated notes and messages to classmates and visitors. As an interactive message board, they post each note in the appropriate alphabet box that corresponds to the designated receiver's name.

Kingore, B. (2011). *Tiered Learning Stations in Minutes.* Austin, TX: PA Publishing.

## *APPLICATION TIME: REFLECT AND SELECT*

# *I have a plan!*

**Planning Tiered Learning stations**

Title: _____

_____

Grade levels: _____        Icon:

Targeted skills and concepts:

- _____

- _____

- _____

Tiered factors:

- _____

- _____

- _____

Equipment–materials:

Ideas for learning experiences:

**Continue your ideas on another page**

Kingore, B. (2011). *Tiered Learning Stations in Minutes*. Austin, TX: PA Publishing.

# *5*
# *Fast Starts for Successful Stations*

## IDEAS THAT WORK

Implement procedures that increase the likelihood for student success during learning station time. We dare not expect students to do well at something with which they have little or no experience. The following suggestions guide the training process, increase student ownership, ease management issues, and simplify the intensity of initiating stations that effectively augment learning opportunities. Skim the ideas and select one or more to help learning stations result in success-filled experiences for students and educators.

### One Station First

Start simply. Begin with one station so students assimilate the process and behaviors as expected routines for learning station times. Concentrating on one station allows practice time for the students to polish the skills required for working independently from the teacher. Add one or more additional stations as students demonstrate that they are ready to understand and apply the routines of station-based learning.

For example, initiate station-based learning with a self-concept or *Thinking About Me* station. Since each person is the expert about herself or himself, the station emphasizes the importance of each person rather than capabilities or readiness differences. Hence, all students have the opportunity to participate successfully while practicing the behaviors and procedures required when learning at stations.

### One Learning Task First

Begin station-based learning with all students completing the same learning experience at a station until they understand the routine. Then, differentiate the tasks in the station to match the students' range of readiness and diversity of learning profiles.

Kingore, B. (2011). *Tiered Learning Stations in Minutes*. Austin, TX: PA Publishing.

**Limit Time**

To help students learn the routines of station-based learning, initially limit the time students spend at a station by using familiar learning experiences that require a minimum of time to complete. A brief period, such as ten minutes, allows students to work at a station while they learn the routines and expectations of station-based learning. As their independent learning skills develop, increase the allotted time by five minutes until reaching the length of time preferred for stations.

**Try-Out Station Routines**

When initiating multiple stations for the first time, provide a training experience on the first  day. Enable students to practice moving among different stations by scheduling only two or three minutes at each location. Students try out the learning stations and the process of changing locations as the teacher directs the procedure.

**Each-One-Teach-One**

Initially, teach one or two students the most effective procedures and behaviors for working at learning stations. Then, each student teaches another until understanding permeates the entire class. This process increases student ownership in learning stations, recognizes peers as resources and support agents, results in only a small number of students in a station during learning time, and is an efficient use of time for the students and the teacher.

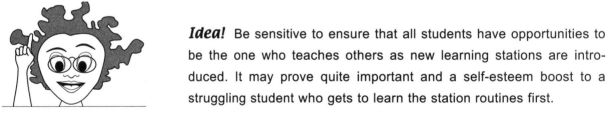

*Idea!* Be sensitive to ensure that all students have opportunities to be the one who teaches others as new learning stations are introduced. It may prove quite important and a self-esteem boost to a struggling student who gets to learn the station routines first.

**Long-term Stations**

Avoid eliminating current stations and initiating different stations too frequently. Creating new stations demands both extensive preparation time and student training time yet may not increase achievement. Instead, develop stations with long-term applications to the curriculum. Retain high interest in station-based learning by using interesting and important learning experiences that elicit student engagement, and then, add or delete a few items each week or so to keep the station experiences varied and fresh.

Kingore, B. (2011). *Tiered Learning Stations in Minutes*. Austin, TX: PA Publishing.

## Student-Created Organizers and Graphics

Involve students in creating organizational aids for learning stations. Students feel more ownership in a station when they assist in its development. Student-created organizers also allow more efficient use of students' time when they work at stations.

✓ Students wrap or decorate cans, containers, and boxes for pencil holders, organizers, and materials.

✓ Students write and decorate station signs, labels, and title posters. They enjoy adding three-dimensional items that are associated with the station, such as math construction tools and attribute block templates.

✓ Students create borders and captions to decorate bulletin boards.

## Peer Assistants

Use students as task assistants and skill assistants who provide support and respond to other students' questions and needs. Peer assistants experience a self-esteem boost as they confidently assist others. In addition, student-to-student collaborations make a positive statement about the class as a community of learners: Classmates have expertise to help one another.

### Task Assistants

Student task assistants are briefly trained by the teacher to be experienced with a specific learning task or product. As individuals or small groups work, the assistant is recognized as one who can answer questions and provide help when needed. Using digital photographs of each student, post the current task assistant's photograph in a designated place in the classroom. The picture is a positive recognition and informs others of the identity of the assistant. Post a picture of different task assistants at more than one station when needed to involve multiple *experts* during station time. Even students with fewer skills can serve as the assistant on selected tasks by meeting with the teacher in advance to learn how to correctly complete that learning experience. All students need multiple opportunities to be task assistants.

### Skill Assistants

Student skill assistants are prepared to help others with specific skills. When applying writing conventions, for example, attach different skills (such as the use of commas, capitalization, or specific spelling patterns) to each pocket of a shoe bag or pocket chart. When students believe they have ample understanding to help others with a skill, they write their names on strips cut from index cards and put the name-strips in the specific skill pocket. If students have questions about a skill, they search that skill pocket for the name of a peer available to help. This technique motivates some students to master a skill so they can enjoy being recognized as an assistant with expertise in that skill.

Kingore, B. (2011). *Tiered Learning Stations in Minutes.* Austin, TX: PA Publishing.

**Pre-experienced Learning Tasks**

In general, use products and learning experiences that have been previously taught to students. If the task has been modeled with the whole class and successfully applied in small groups, individuals are more likely to experience success without needing assistance. For example, once students have experience with Venn diagrams, they are more likely to successfully apply the diagrams to different topics at a station. In most cases, an engaging learning experience that students have successfully experienced in the past becomes a viable choice for independent application at a learning station. Obviously, vary the application of the learning experience to retain student enthusiasm.

**Think Time**

Use learning experiences that require prolonged thinking and planning. Think time engages high-level thinking, increases attention spans, and encourages higher-level responses. Plan learning experiences that emphasize the head rather than the hand as some children's hands wear out before their heads. For example, many concept maps require a minimum of writing yet demand high-level thinking to generate an original response.

*Idea!* Tiered, open-ended learning experiences at appropriate levels of challenge capture students' interests and attention longer than simple matching or fill-in-the-blank tasks.

**Books and Commercial Materials**

Veteran teachers find it productive to review children's literature, the internet, and commercial task cards to glean ready-to-use station items. Evaluate all types of commercially available materials and equipment for those that meaningfully integrate essential learning objectives. Seek materials that positively present and integrate social and language diversity.

**Nonfiction Materials**

Develop stations that incorporate vast quantities of nonfiction materials. Obtain these materials from school and public libraries to place in classroom stations. Students request nonfiction information that enables them to learn more about personal topics of interest including past or present cultures, animal

Kingore, B. (2011). *Tiered Learning Stations in Minutes*. Austin, TX: PA Publishing.

species, technology, and specific events including historical moments and scientific phenomenon such as volcanic eruptions.

### Exploration Experiences

Exploration precedes application. When introducing new materials at a station, allow students to handle and explore the materials for a while before introducing learning task requirements. For example, when young children first discover geoboards and rubber bands at a math station, they want to experiment using the boards. Be insightful and allow opportunities for discovery and experimentation before including specific geometric patterns for children to reproduce. After exploration experiences, children are better prepared to complete assigned learning tasks.

### Use of Equipment

Assist students in the appropriate use of equipment. Students need freedom to explore applications, but they also need direction when a specific procedure or product is expected. For example, a student who has not used a microscope benefits from someone modeling how to load a slide onto the stage and focus the objective lens.

*Idea!* Use a student assistant who remains at one station for an appropriate period of time to demonstrate to others how to use new equipment.

## INSTANT APPEAL

### Simple Things that Amplify Interest

Simple, readily available items can add a spark to several learning stations. The following list may prompt brainstorming of additional effective choices to quickly increase the appeal of stations.

> ✓ Aquarium
> ✓ Bean bag or inflatable chair
> ✓ Cardboard box–large enough so a student can go inside
> ✓ Clip boards
> ✓ Feely box
> ✓ Flashlight
> ✓ Individual chalkboards or wipe-off boards

✓ Inflatables

✓ Jewelry

✓ Lamp

✓ Magnifying glass

✓ Manipulatives

✓ Mirror

✓ Music

✓ Note pads

✓ Photographs

✓ Picture frame with a stand—Contains a feature article, captivating picture, news, or announcements

✓ Pillows

✓ Plants

✓ Recording device

✓ Rubber stamp

✓ Sheet (over a table)

✓ Sleeping bag

✓ Stress balls and silent squeezing toys

✓ Stickers

✓ Stuffed animals

✓ Technology

✓ Treasure chest

✓ Visor

## Visual Attractions

Simple graphics can be used year-round to add visual appeal and continuity to classroom displays, bulletin boards, and stations. The alphabet figures, numeral figures, and polygon figures on the Tool Box CD are creative visuals that connect whimsical appeal to the concepts and skills in math and language arts. They can be used as manipulatives, borders, or decorative accents in a variety of colors and sizes. Using these figures in multiple stations provides a unifying visual element throughout the classroom.

Kingore, B. (2011). *Tiered Learning Stations in Minutes*. Austin, TX: PA Publishing.

Icons that graphically represent different stations are visually appealing and provide an effective communication device. When these icons are posted around the classroom, young children, ELL, and struggling students use beginning reading skills to interpret the icons and recognize the various station locations.

**Look Alikes**

**Editor's Office**

The Tool Box CD includes two sizes of the learning station icons—the small size pictured here and an enlarged version. The CD also provides the icons in colors and in black and white to increase application possibilities. Teachers are encouraged to enlarge the icons further to increase applications, such as icons large enough to view from across the room or become part of a decoration on a station sign. On the Tool Box CD, there are icons for the twenty tiered learning stations in minutes and the twelve station ideas especially proposed for young learners in this chapter. These learning stations exemplify frequent station choices that relate to curriculum and essential learning standards in today's classrooms.

Kingore, B. (2011). *Tiered Learning Stations in Minutes*. Austin, TX: PA Publishing.

# APPLICATION TIME:
# REFLECT AND SELECT

## Racing Toward Success

To quickly initiate success-filled stations, I will:

- - - - - - - - - - - - - - -

These ideas are particularly important considerations for stations for young learners:

**Finish line!**

- - - - - - - - - - - - - - -

I can add instant appeal to stations by:

Kingore, B. (2011). *Tiered Learning Stations in Minutes*. Austin, TX: PA Publishing.

# Organizing Learning Stations

## · 6 ·

## HOW MANY STUDENTS? HOW MANY STATIONS? HOW OFTEN?

> *Provide the appropriate kind and number of stations*
> *for essential learning objectives,*
> *room size, arrangement, and number of students.*

**How many students?** Research suggests that groups of two to four students increase active participation, mental engagement and achievement. Embrace the objective of groups of two to four at learning stations, but understand that when the quantity of available stations requires larger groups, students can regroup at the station and work in pairs or trios to still encourage the higher achievement facilitated by small group interactions.

Determine the specific number of students at any station by assessing how many students the station location and materials accommodate. The intent is to organize a small group who can interact for idea sharing and work productively at the same time. For example, if there are three computers, the station supports three students unless the effect of the software program or learning task is enhanced by students cooperatively sharing a computer. If there is space at a writing station for four chairs, then four students could be involved. When space and equipment allow, the simplest process is to have the same number of students at each location, such as four per station. This arrangement is easy for students to remember.

**How many stations?** The follow equation represents the number of learning stations needed to foster achievement.

$$\text{The number of stations} = \frac{\text{The total number of students at stations at the same time}}{\text{The number of students preferred at each station}}$$

If all students are at stations at the same time, the stations must have room for the total number of students in the class. Provide space for the number of students who will work at each station

Kingore, B. (2011). *Tiered Learning Stations in Minutes*. Austin, TX: PA Publishing.

at one time plus an extra space or two to allow students to change stations when they complete the learning task. In other words, in a class of twenty-nine children, approximately thirty-two station spaces are needed. If four students are to be at a learning stations at one time, then eight stations are required.

However, all students are not necessarily at stations at the same time. For example, some students might work with the teacher as others work independently at their seats and others work in stations. In a room of twenty-seven children, if a third of the students are at stations at a time, then spaces for nine children are needed. This scenario requires only three stations with three or four students in each.

**How often?** Teachers wonder how often to use stations. In the majority of classrooms that employ station-based learning, students work at stations every day. However, instructional objectives differ, so some classes may only utilize stations once or twice a week. In a middle school class, for example, the teacher might elect to use whole-class instruction for three days a week, cooperative learning applications for one day, and learning station applications for the fifth day each week. During learning station times, the teacher has the opportunity to briefly pull together small groups for reteaching or extensions of learning that respond to students' readiness.

## ORGANIZATION MODELS

There are several ways to organize a station-based learning environment, and each model is potentially effective. The best choice depends upon instructional objectives, curriculum, teacher preferences, and consideration of the students' best ways to learn. The models also differ in the balance between teacher-control and student autonomy, so some models initially prove better for students who have less experience and lack independent learning skills.

In the first three models that follow, the teacher directly teaches one group of students while others participate in varied, assigned tasks during learning station time. The objectives of this organization are teacher-directed instruction with a small group and flexible grouping applications. The teacher is mainly involved with one group at a time while maintaining a visual survey of the other students at work in other locations. During transition times, the teacher can interact briefly with groups or individual students.

In the final two models, the teacher simultaneously facilitates all groups during learning station time. The objective of this organization is assessment and evaluation of students during flexible group learning experiences. The teacher is mainly involved in observation, writing anecdotal records, and completing assessments of students' skills and achievement. The teacher engages with students in spontaneous learning moments, encourages, and redirects behavior as needed as students work at stations.

Kingore, B. (2011). *Tiered Learning Stations in Minutes*. Austin, TX: PA Publishing.

***Caution!*** Change group membership frequently so different students experience working in different groups.

### 1. One-Third Model

With the one-third model, the teacher assigns the group memberships and controls the sequence and schedule of station-based learning time. One-third of the class works with the teacher in a guided learning group, one-third completes independent work, and one-third works in stations. Two or three stations are sufficient because this model only requires spaces for one-third of the class at a time. Scheduled for twenty or thirty minutes each, station-based learning, independent work, and guided instruction with the teacher are completed in an hour or one and one-half hour block of time with students rotating among the three options. All students participate in all three learning formats each day and experience all of the different stations by the end of the week.

The one-third model is an effective follow-up to whole class instruction. While directing a lesson with the entire class, the teacher provides the introductory information, examples, and modeling that benefits all students. The teacher can also demonstrate and assign a learning task for students to practice and complete independently at a later time. The class then commences with the one-third model, thus, making it possible for the teacher to differentiate the materials, concepts, and skills appropriately for each group during their guided learning with the teacher.

### 2. Daily Rotation Model

With the daily rotation model, the teacher assigns the group memberships and controls the sequence and schedule of station-based learning time. When completing instruction with one group, the teacher sounds a signal, and all groups rotate clock-wise to the next station. Depending upon the total number of students in the class, there are five or six stations in the room, including the one directed by the teacher. (Some teachers are successful using four stations for daily rotation. However, the number of students in each station escalates in order to accommodate all of the class.) All students rotate through all stations each day. Using six stations, the total learning time lasts for one and one-half hours with fifteen minutes per station, or two hours with twenty minutes per station.

### 3. Planning Board Model

The planning board model encourages the greatest degree of student autonomy. With this model, students control the pace and sequence of station-based learning while also having some input in the group membership. A planning board, described and illustrated later in this section, displays all of the available stations in the room. Students go to the planning board and select a station. When they have completed quality work, they return to the planning board and select another station.

Kingore, B. (2011). *Tiered Learning Stations in Minutes*. Austin, TX: PA Publishing.

As students work at stations, the teacher selects groups of students to instruct in a teacher-directed lesson, such as guided reading or math instruction. Depending on allotted time, the teacher works with each group each day or three to four times a week. Learning station time lasts for 45 minutes to one hour or more.

### 4. One-Station-a-Day Rotation

With the one-station-a-day model, the teacher divides the class into five groups, assigns the group memberships, and controls the sequence and schedule of station-based learning time. Every day, each group is assigned to a different station so that by the end of the week, all five stations have been visited by each student. During learning station time, the teacher moves among the groups to observe, facilitate, and assess.

Five stations are required as student groups rotate to a different station each day. Since all groups participate in stations at the same time, the teacher provides sufficient places at each station to accommodate one-fifth of the total class. This model requires 20 or 30 minutes of daily class time.

### 5. Variation of Planning Board Model

Similar to the planning board model, this variation enables students to control the pace and sequence of station-based learning time while also having some input in the group membership. Multiple stations are listed on a planning board and students select among them to complete a designated number of different stations by the end of one or two weeks. When individual students have completed quality work at one station, they return to the planning board and select another station. As all students work in stations, the teacher moves among the groups to facilitate learning and assess students' skill applications and achievement. Learning station time lasts for 30 to 45 minutes a day.

*Caution!* Avoid an organization model in which student only enter stations after they complete their other work as that model has negative potential.

1. It may prevent struggling students or contemplative students from ever having time to experience stations.
2. It might encourage a lower quality of work from some students inclined to rush through regular assignments so they can get to stations.
3. It signals that stations are fun rewards instead of essential learning objectives.

## STUDENT PLACEMENT

There are many ways to direct students into learning stations. Four examples follow to prompt a decision of which one would be the most effective application.

Kingore, B. (2011). *Tiered Learning Stations in Minutes*. Austin, TX: PA Publishing.

## Morning Meetings

Many elementary classes begin each day with a whole-group discussion and application of numerous skills. At the closure of the morning group time, the teacher or a child randomly selects students' name sticks. As each name is drawn, that child chooses a station and places the name stick in a decorated container at that station. That station remains available for others to select until the number of students' names in the container totals the number allowed in that station.

The random nature of drawing names makes this method seem equitable.

However, to prevent students from overusing the same stations, techniques for students' record keeping should be added to this method.

***Caution!*** This method requires several minutes to get students settled into stations. Time is wasted as some children look around to make a decision.

## Rotation Posters

Rotation methods maintain the greatest teacher control. The teacher pre-assigns students to groups based upon mixed-readiness, similar readiness, or interests. By frequently changing group memberships, the teacher limits stagnant groups and negative labeling. At teacher-directed times, the groups rotate among the stations in a predetermined sequence. On a poster, position cards with groups of students' names to designate in which station each group is to begin working. For example, children review a merry-go-round poster to determine which station their group is assigned. Each day, assign a different station to each group so that after a few days, all students have experienced all of the learning stations. Student choice is provided by the variety of activities within each station.

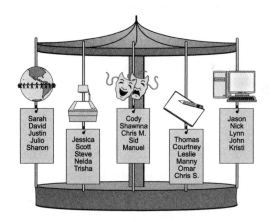

## Contracts

Contracts provide opportunities for students to work independently with some freedom while maintaining the teacher's instructional objectives. This differentiation tool integrates student goal setting and record keeping. Some expected behaviors and learning tasks may be duplicated on all students' contracts. Other behaviors and tasks may be unique to one student or one group of students in response to particular assessed needs.

Kingore, B. (2011). *Tiered Learning Stations in Minutes*. Austin, TX: PA Publishing.

Contracts increase student responsibility while the teacher facilitates. Typically, contracts enable students to choose the sequence in which they complete stations and manage the length of time they spend at each station. Students are free to make many choices and decisions regarding their completion of designated learning experiences as long as they fulfill the terms of their contracts. (The Tool Box CD includes examples of student contracts.)

*Idea!* Limit introductory explanations. Avoid beginning the week with explanations that require students to sit and watch as the teacher goes around the stations providing introductory information. This process takes too long, children's attention diminishes, and there is no student involvement in learning. Avoid lengthy introductions by incorporating previously taught learning experiences and using students as task and skill assistants.

## Planning Board

A planning board empowers students to proceed more independently within the learning environment. It displays representations of all the classroom learning stations and requires students to plan their use of station time. Students refer to the planning board and select stations to work in during learning station time. Whenever they have completed the station learning experiences and have demonstrated quality work, they have the right to return to the planning board and select another station in which to continue their learning. Students select different stations rather than just repeating a favorite because they understand that they must complete a designated number of different stations by the end of one or two weeks.

With a planning board, students are responsible for both the sequence they work at specific stations and their pace of learning as they determine the duration of time required for them to complete station learning experiences. They may also choose of the some classmates they work with because peers can make plans to work together before they select a station. A planning board eliminates the problem of some children finishing earlier and having to wait for others in the group to complete the tasks or having to wait until the teacher signals that is time to change or conclude stations. With a planning board, students complete quality work in a station and then place themselves in a different station.

The illustrated clothespin board is an example of a planning board. It displays an icon for each station and has a short length of wide yarn with clothespins attached under each icon. The number of clothespins designates the number of students who can work in that station at one time. Prepare the planning board by copying each icon in a different color that is coordinated to match the colors of the clothespins. As an alternative, glue each paper icon on a paper that frames the icon in a different color to match that color of the spray-painted clothespins.

Kingore, B. (2011). *Tiered Learning Stations in Minutes*. Austin, TX: PA Publishing.

Students scan the planning board, select a station in which to work, and attach the corresponding clothespin to their clothing. The color makes it easy to identify which of the students are supposed to be at each station. When children complete the station learning tasks, they return the clothespin to the planning board and select another station.

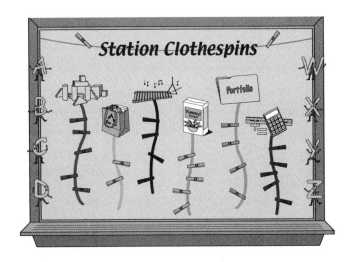

As a variation, create a planning board with station icons and a hook for laminated paper keys underneath each. Students' names are on the keys. To select a station, students hang their name key under the icon. Teachers write a number beside each station icon to denote how many may work in that station.

Planning boards encourage student responsibility and decision making. This organization model allows flexibility in the sequence in which students complete designated

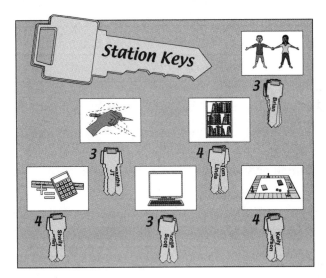

stations and the amount of time each child needs to successfully complete the learning tasks. Teachers report fewer discipline problems when students have choices and determine their own place and pace. As one secondary teacher expressed: "They learn more and you manage less" (Tedrow, 2008).

## Combinations Over Time

Over time, combinations of different methods for placing students in stations may prove useful. For example, a teacher might initiate station experiences with teacher-directed rotation in order to maintain control, establish station routines, and provide time for students to increase their self-management skills. Later, the teacher can initiate a planning board as well as student record keeping to increase learners' choices, responsibilities, and development of the skills of autonomous students.

Kingore, B. (2011). *Tiered Learning Stations in Minutes*. Austin, TX: PA Publishing.

## *SIGNALS AND TRANSITIONS*

Students do not change gears effortlessly. They need to be informed ahead of time that it is almost time for a change so they can bring closure to their current task. Establish different signals to represent reoccurring messages. For example, use signals that inform students when attention is needed and when to begin or end tasks. Once established, signals save class time because fewer directions need to be verbalized. They become a part of the routine that produces smoother, quieter transitions.

Establish an attention signal for students to be quiet and listen. As a class, determine a simple signal to use when immediate attention is needed, such as when an announcement is made or a refocus is required. Examples of effective signals include flicking the lights, ringing a bell, clap patterns, hands raised and held in place, and verbal statements, such as: *When you hear my voice, snap* [fingers snap one time]. Flicking the lights is often the fastest way to achieve total attention but has the disadvantage of location since one has to be close to the light switch to initiate the signal.

Signals facilitate students' time management. Create a three-minute warning signal to prepare students by letting them know that limited time remains. This signal informs them that it is time to reach closure with their activities and clean up or reorganize the station area. If using a rotation method, issue a rotation signal three minutes after the closure signal so students understand to rotate to another station or exit the station and return to their desks.

When learning station time concludes, initiate a transition activity that is interesting and engaging. This procedure gives students a reason to conclude station activities in a timely manner. A student-directed activity works especially well at this time so the teacher is free to facilitate, oversee the closure of station activities, and briefly interact with individual students.

### Signal and Transition Examples

1.  **Lights**

    As a visual signal with an immediate effect, flash the lights on and off, and repeat if needed.

2.  **Sound**

    Issue a sound signal with a xylophone run, bell, clap pattern, or musical chord. For example, three claps indicate that three minutes remain. If a signal begins to lose its value, more inventive sounds should be substituted, such as an ah-ooga horn or whistle. Vocal sounds might also be used as signals, however, they are easier to ignore and may prove less effective.

3.  **Music CDs**

    Music is often a welcomed addition to the classroom. Using a remote control, activate a selection from a CD of music that is established as the signal piece. Use the same musical selection

Kingore, B. (2011). *Tiered Learning Stations in Minutes*. Austin, TX: PA Publishing.

repeatedly so students understand: *When you hear this music...* Specifically, plan a three-minute segment of the music to signal the beginning and conclusion of learning station time. When it begins to play, students know to go to learning stations or to begin cleaning up and reorganizing the station. As children become familiar with the segment, they learn to pace themselves so they appropriately begin or finish as the music ends.

Consider using classical selections for this signal to expose children to a wider variety of music. Remember that the brain research indicates classical music with its more complex structures, especially the compositions of Mozart and Bach, helps to temporarily increase brain activity. Change the selection monthly so children are exposed to many different compositions.

## 4. Announce and Pause

Announce the intended behavior and tell students when to proceed. *In two seconds, you may quietly move to your station. (*Pause.) *Begin.* This signal gives students a second to process the information before acting upon it.

## 5. Countdown

In primary classrooms, lead students in an oral countdown as a beginning and ending signal.

## 6. Chant

When students rotate among stations, use the simple chant: *2-4-6-8* (clap) *rotate.*

## 7. Debriefing

Debriefing helps students process and retain information. For the last minute or so of a station, initiate debriefing as a closure task among the students at each station. *Tell one person at the station about something you worked on or completed today.* (Pause) *Now, switch parts.*

## 8. Transition Songs

When working with young children, create transition songs by substituting information messages as the words to well-know tunes. Primary children enjoy the familiarity of the song and quickly join in the singing.

- Transition for ending station time:

  (Tune: "Mulberry Bush" - Three minutes before concluding stations)

  *IT'S TIME TO PUT THE STATIONS AWAY,*

  *STATIONS AWAY, STATIONS AWAY.*

  *IT'S TIME TO PUT THE STATIONS AWAY,*

  *WE'LL WORK IN THEM ANOTHER DAY.*

- Transition for station rotations:

  (Tune: "Mulberry Bush" - When time for rotation)

  *ROUND AND ROUND THE stations WE GO.*

  *IT'S TIME TO MOVE TO THE NEXT IN THE ROW.*

Kingore, B. (2011). *Tiered Learning Stations in Minutes.* Austin, TX: PA Publishing.

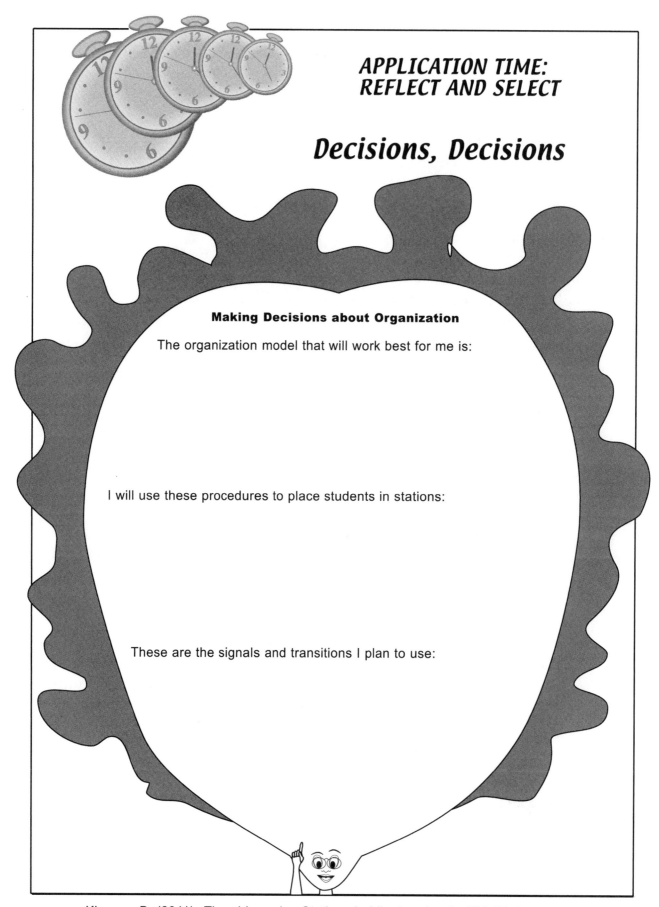

APPLICATION TIME:
REFLECT AND SELECT

## Decisions, Decisions

### Making Decisions about Organization

The organization model that will work best for me is:

I will use these procedures to place students in stations:

These are the signals and transitions I plan to use:

# *Ensuring Productivity*

## *ESTABLISH ROUTINES*

Effective teachers establish classroom routines that enable themselves and their students to work productively and efficiently. Routines arm students with the parameters of station-based learning so they understand expectations and procedures. Once established, routines permit teachers to instruct small groups or conference with individuals, assured that the rest of the class can and will proceed productively with their learning responsibilities.

Initially, work with students to establish routines so that productivity and organization become a habit. Making these decisions together increases students' ownership in the classroom and shares responsibility to ensure that everything proceeds as planned. The predictability of routines frees students to relax and focus their energy on learning. Ideally, class routines are organized yet flexible as occasional change is refreshing.

To establish routines, students should role play routines for daily learning tasks. Role-playing matches many students' best ways to learn as they actively demonstrate understanding through auditory, kinesthetic, and visual modalities. Furthermore, role play connects students' interest in creative dramatics and the performing arts. Role play learning station routines, such as interacting with peers, documenting the quality of their work, working quietly, cleaning up, displaying work, and moving between learning locations. Children exhibit significantly fewer behavior management problems during their time at learning stations when they have participated in practice sessions through role play and class discussions. For example, all class members literally walk through a simulation of how to appropriately use a rubric to self-assess their work and then reorganize the station before leaving.

*Idea!* As an engaging switch, an adult role plays a student working in stations. The students watch and offer suggestions to improve what is being done incorrectly.

---

Kingore, B. (2011). *Tiered Learning Stations in Minutes*. Austin, TX: PA Publishing.

**Getting Materials**

Since students complete work at different times, allow individuals to be responsible for getting their own materials as needed. As a class, establish when and how to get materials and determine storage locations with a place for everything and everything in its place. This routine prevents students from having to wait as a few helpers pass things out, avoids teachers doing it all, and makes better use of class time. Throughout the day, this procedure is also a welcomed movement for bodily-kinesthetic learners.

*Idea!* Label the learning environment. When appropriate, label materials and storage with words and symbols so young and special-needs children have prior experience and graphic support to successfully read the labels and manage materials well.

**Documenting Quality**

Develop routines that actively involve students in self assessing the quality of their work. As a class, have students role play and practice using a rubric every day to self-assess the learning behaviors they demonstrate by their work at stations. Establish the routine of students recording this assessment and writing reflections about learning experiences in their daily station logs as a closure to station-based learning. The Tool Box CD contains several examples of learning behavior rubrics and station log templates at varying levels of complexity for very young, elementary, and middle school students.

**Reorganizing Stations**

Model clean-up procedures as a class routine. Students come to understand that clean-up and the reorganization of materials is a learning responsibility required anytime they use shared materials or equipment. This routine has life value as organization and maintaining order are assets in most working situations.

**Completing Transitions**

Transitions are a key part of interactive classrooms. Students move from one learning location to another and shift from one group configuration to another. To promote efficiency, teachers and students preplan transition routines, determine transition signals, role play foot-traffic patterns, and arrange classroom furniture so movement is efficient rather than disruptive.

---

Kingore, B. (2011). *Tiered Learning Stations in Minutes*. Austin, TX: PA Publishing.

## MINI-LESSONS

If behavioral difficulties occur while implementing learning stations, conduct a brief mini-lesson and problem-solve with the class to elicit ways to resolve the conflict while ensuring student ownership in the solutions. Involving the students in the discussion will increase their motivation and effectiveness in their independent learning.

> **Mini-Lesson Topics**
> Completing quality work
> Interrupting peers or the teacher
> Using the planning board
> Working quietly and responsibly
> Using materials or equipment appropriately
> Transitioning between learning locations
> Reorganizing when station time ends
> Getting needed materials
> Posting completed work
> Cooperating with others in stations
> Completing self-assessments accurately
> Maintaining station logs
> Interacting with task or skill assistants
> Responding to signals

## QUALITY: DEFINED AND MODELED

Inspire students to aspire to produce quality work as a personal goal and source of pride. In prior learning environments, students may have misconstrued that being correct, neat, and on time were the valued criteria. While those attributes are important, guide students to understand that quality work and continuous learning are the class targets. Class time spent discussing and defining quality can increase students' commitment to excellence.

✓ **Demonstrate both high-quality and lower-quality products.**
Help students formulate more concrete targets for quality by providing examples of learning responses that range from weak to strong. When appropriate, provide a product rubric and facilitate as students discuss the criteria and work together using the rubric to evaluate the high-quality and lower-quality products presented as examples.

Kingore, B. (2011). *Tiered Learning Stations in Minutes*. Austin, TX: PA Publishing.

***Caution!*** Invest time in thoroughly training students to use rubrics. Providing a rubric to students before beginning an assignment is necessary but insufficient to support learning. Students may lack the teacher's clear conception of what constitutes quality work (McTighe & O'Conner, 2005).

✓ **Analyze the attributes of quality.**

Guide the class in defining quality by brainstorming a list of the attributes that result in quality work. Then, students refine the attributes into a Top Ten List. Students clarify their thinking about quality as they reach consensus regarding the hierarchy of the attributes.

✓ **Develop a rubric for high-quality products.**

With upper elementary and middle school classes, work together to develop a generalizable rubric that communicates clear criteria for quality products and learning responses that promote high achievement so that students understand what is expected of them. For example, the rubric might progress from *flawed information,* to *accurate basic information,* to *thoughtful information and details,* to *in-depth, clearly supported information.*

✓ **Actively follow through on the accuracy of students' self evaluations.**

Conduct a mini-lesson if the accurate assessment of quality is a whole class issue. If only one or two students have accuracy issues, meet with each individual to briefly review specific use of a self-assessment rubric. Ask involved students to justify each level they self-assessed on the rubric with specific examples in their products. Actively listen and clarify when misunderstandings exist.

✓ **Establish a reason for quality.**

Plan with students how to share work with authentic audiences. Examples of several options follow.

- Post the work for others to view.
- Teach the process or product to a younger student.
- Share the work orally during class discussions.
- Discuss the work in a small group of peers. *Tell each other one thing you did well in stations today. Share one idea or goal for tomorrow's station work.*
- Share products with someone at home. Requesting a brief written response from whomever reviews the work may add even more importance and long-term enjoyment to the process.

✓ **Communicate directions and realistic expectations.**

Quality is more likely when students clearly understand directions and expectations before beginning station-based learning. When advisable, provide both verbal and written directions to accommodate diverse learning modalities and eliminate confusion. Communicating realistic expectations is vital as students are more compelled to make an effort to learn when they perceive that success is likely (Sullo, 2009).

***Idea!*** *Record directions.* During whole-class instruction, simultaneously make an audio recording of explanations of procedures, directions, and expectations for stations and independent work. Make the recording available to students who need to listen a second time and to students who return after being absent.

## *TECHNIQUES FOR NOISE CONTROL*

✓ **Concretely establish the preferred range of volume.**

As a class, discuss a *productive buzz* of sound versus the roar of *chaos*. Involve the class in role playing the different levels of sound on a continuum from *productive learning level* to *out of control*. Noise problems tend to reoccur, so be prepared to revisit earlier discussions. Actively involve the class in role playing and problem solving again if needed.

✓ **Elicit students' ideas.**

Students have more ownership in noise control when they participate in establishing the parameters. Furthermore, adults benefit from understanding students' perspectives of what is excessive and why excessive noises occur. Predictably, students' perception may differ dramatically from an adult perspective.

✓ **Talk softly whenever possible.**

After securing students' attention, many teachers effectively lower the volume of their voice and proceed with a quieter, more personal message. A soft voice exudes calm and often causes students to listen more carefully. Conversely, as adults increase their volume, so do others in the room.

***Idea!*** With young learners, keep a puppet or small stuffed animal in a pocket or drawer as a class figure or mascot. Explain to the children that the selected figure wants to take a nap during station work. As stations begin, announce to the class: *Work quietly so we do not disturb _____'s rest.* At the conclusion of station time, the puppet or animal reappears to thank the children for the quiet nap time and share other specific and positive comments about their work.

Kingore, B. (2011). *Tiered Learning Stations in Minutes.* Austin, TX: PA Publishing.

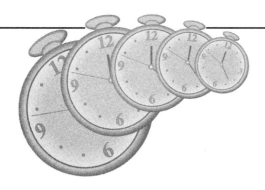

*APPLICATION TIME:*
*REFLECT AND SELECT*

*Concept Map*

| **Routines to Establish:** | **How to Model Quality:** |
| --- | --- |
| | |

**Ensuring Productivity**

| **Ideas for Noise Control:** | **Additional Ideas:** |
| --- | --- |
| | |

Kingore, B. (2011). *Tiered Learning Stations in Minutes*. Austin, TX: PA Publishing.

# The Teacher's Roles

The teacher is a significant influence on students' level of achievement, determining and directing the process that enables students to experience continuous learning (NAEYC & NAECS/SDE, 2003; Stronge, 2002). Effective teachers recognize, respect, and respond to student differences. In doing so, they create a lasting effect on students' lives.

The teacher is the facilitator of learning and key decision maker in the classroom. To facilitate learning, teachers assume many different roles during the class time devoted to learning stations. As decision makers, teachers select the learning tasks that promote achievement gains and determine the parameters that enable a productive learning environment.

## FACILITATOR OF LEARNING

A teacher's enthusiasm for teaching and respect for students is contagious when teachers incorporate station-based learning to engage students in meaningful learning applications. As students work at learning stations, teachers demonstrate many different roles in response to specific instructional objectives. The following options are typical of the ways teachers facilitate learning during the class time devoted to learning stations.

### Assessment

The purpose of assessment is to guide instruction and benefit learners. When all children participate in stations at the same time, teachers facilitate, observe, and assess students as they work and participate in station tasks. Teachers assess the skill levels and applications students exhibit as they work. Conversations among students during stations provide many assessment opportunities and reveal the *process* as well as the *products* of learning. Listening to what children say as they work provides insight into their schema and level of achievement. Many teachers determine extension or reteaching needs based upon these assessments during stations. Simple skills checklists, such as those found on the Tool Box CD, are useful to guide teachers' observations and notes.

Kingore, B. (2011). *Tiered Learning Stations in Minutes*. Austin, TX: PA Publishing.

For assessment purposes, carry a small writing pad when walking among station groups. Jot down quick notes to document observations and assessments of students' capabilities and needs.

*Idea!* Writing notes while moving among the groups piques students' self-awareness. Students may ask: *What are you writing?* My most effective response is: *Things I need to remember about you and your work.* Students are not exactly sure what that means and usually get back on task quickly.

### Direct Instruction

Many teachers use the station time as an opportunity to directly instruct one small group of students at a time. This role enables teachers to work with groups of students at their different instructional levels. As the teacher works with one group to guide their instruction, the rest of the students participate in stations. After several minutes of instruction, the teacher dismisses that group for independent work or station time. The teacher then proceeds to directly instruct another group at their instructional level. This process continues so all students receive the level of instruction that enables continuous learning.

*Idea!* Sometimes, disruptions occur within a station when the teacher is directly teaching another group. If the situation does not risk students' bodily harm, write quick notes of the problem to address when finished directly teaching the current group. Recording the problem for later action prevents an interruption to instruction and saves the valuable time of the current group.

### Conference

Teachers can choose to conference, problem solve, and plan with specific students as the rest of the students participate in stations. Large numbers of mini-conferences can be accomplished in this manner. Arrange "appointments" with students before station time to avoid a student being in a station and not wanting to or not being able to stop.

### Coach

Teachers interact with individuals or very small groups of children during station time to coach, facilitate, and encourage achievement. Teachers might say to a student working in a station: *What can you teach us about this today? Everyone has something to teach us if we listen.*

---

Kingore, B. (2011). *Tiered Learning Stations in Minutes*. Austin, TX: PA Publishing.

Teachers pose questions to students to prompt their high-level thinking and process aware-ness. Questions and statements such as the following are typical of the metacognitive prompts used by effective teachers as they coach learners.

* *Tell me about your work.*
* *What is the hardest part?*
* *How did you figure that out?*
* *What are you going to do next?*
* *What might you do if that does not work out?*

Rather than solely commenting on the correctness of responses, research supports the impor-tance of providing feedback and encouraging children's efforts to achieve and make progress (Dweck, 2007; Sullo, 2009). Students need to believe that their effort leads to success. Teacher feedback in the form of statements similar to the following is productive when coaching and interacting with stu-dents in challenging learning situations.

* *You are on task. Your efforts are working. You are understanding it more now.*
* *You are working to learn this and it shows.*

### Intervene

Teachers can use station time to address special needs and work one-to-one with a student for a few minutes. While teachers frequently spend these special opportunities with struggling stu-dents, it is also possible to work briefly with one or more advanced children to extend their learning challenges. Cleverly, teachers interchangeably intervene with struggling students, advanced learners, and children requiring behavior modifications so intervention occasions are not strictly associated with negative connotations.

Effectively use proximity as a management tool. As needed, move near groups who need a reminder or refocus.

As another type of intervention, assist a child who is having trouble entering into a group's activity during station time. Help establish an assignment or needed role for the child to assume. For example, during role play in Actor's Place, introduce the child as someone who has come to visit.

### Combine Roles

In reality, teachers incorporate combinations of all of these roles during stations. For example, many teachers find it productive to direct instruction on four days and conduct mini-conferences and more specific assessment on the fifth day each week. Effective teachers flexibly respond to the capa-bilities and needs of their students.

Kingore, B. (2011). *Tiered Learning Stations in Minutes*. Austin, TX: PA Publishing.

## DECISION MAKER:
* ### SELECTING APPROPRIATE LEARNING EXPERIENCES FOR STATIONS
* ### ESTABLISHING PRODUCTIVE LEARNING STATIONS

Providing station tasks at appropriate tiers of complexity is essential to the success of students working at learning stations. Tiered learning tasks are vital to students' continuous learning and achievement. Additionally, appropriately challenging learning tasks have a major effect on classroom management and students' learning disposition. When learning tasks are too simple, students lose interest, express boredom, and develop less productive habits of mind, such as not paying attention as they think that everything is easy. When learning tasks are too challenging, students become frustrated and decide that there is no point in trying as they are not going to be able to succeed. They avoid completing the assignment and are at risk to conclude that they are less capable of achievement. In both cases, little or no achievement occurs and behavior problems increase.

A range of tiered learning experiences at stations provide students choice, and choice is a powerful motivator. Some students proceed with more autonomy and exert greater effort when provided task choices (Tedrow, 2008). Rather than all children completing the same task at a station, endeavor to include an appropriate variety of stimulating tasks tiered at different levels of complexity to sustain students' interests and respond to their learning capabilities. To better honor diverse learning profiles and respond to diverse readiness levels, provide a variety of tiered tasks from which students select.

Select learning tasks that target essential academic concepts and skills related to current topics. View standards as springboards for discussions and learning experiences instead of ends in themselves. Effective teachers skillfully integrate clusters of learning standards in engaging tasks that enable students to demonstrate understanding.

### Idea!

*Be not afraid of going slowly;*
*be afraid only of standing still.*
—Anonymous

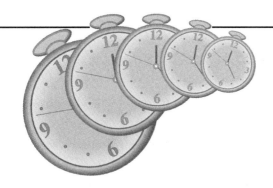

## APPLICATION TIME: REFLECT AND SELECT

### Selecting Appropriate Learning Experiences for Stations

**Yes  No**

☐   ☐   Are all of the learning experiences developmentally appropriate and matched to students' capabilities?

☐   ☐   Are all task choices equitable and appealing to students? Resentment from students is likely if some tasks are perceived as more fun and others as quite laborious.

In what ways do the tasks activate students' mental engagement in learning?

• How are they visually appealing and engaging for visual-spatial learners?

_____

_____

• How do they incorporate bodily-kinesthetic learning?

_____

_____

• How can auditory learners learn through these experiences?

_____

_____

In what ways are these learning tasks meaningful and authentic?

• How are the tasks related to students' backgrounds and readiness levels?

_____

_____

• How do they apply to the diversity of personal interests so students find the tasks interesting and enjoyable?

_____

_____

• Which targeted learning standards, concepts, and skills are integrated into the learning experiences?

_____

_____

Kingore, B. (2011). *Tiered Learning Stations in Minutes*. Austin, TX: PA Publishing.

- How do the tasks enable students to know, understand, and be able to use needed concepts and skills?

  _____

  _____


❑   ❑   Can students successfully complete these activities without the teacher's direct involvement?

❑   ❑   Do the learning experiences vary in complexity so students have opportunities to learn grade-level content but also extend learning beyond that level?

❑   ❑   Is the time required to complete the learning experiences appropriate for a station task?

Which elements of tiered instruction are incorporated so that the complexity levels of the tasks match students' different levels of readiness?

❑   ❑   Background knowledge and skills

❑   ❑   Support system

❑   ❑   Structure of the process

❑   ❑   Concrete or abstract thinking

❑   ❑   Resources

❑   ❑   Complexity of product

How does the design of these tasks increase attention spans?
- What amount of think-time is required of the students?

  _____

  _____

- What degree of paper work is required?

  _____

  _____

- What is their visual appeal?

  _____

  _____

In what ways are academic vocabulary, problem solving, and high-level thinking encouraged by the learning experiences?

  _____

  _____

Kingore, B. (2011). *Tiered Learning Stations in Minutes*. Austin, TX: PA Publishing.

# APPLICATION TIME: REFLECT AND SELECT

## Establishing Productive Learning Stations

What combinations of the following are most effective to share initial instruction or directions with the class?

❑ Whole-class oral instructions

❑ Posted written instructions

❑ Rebus charts and instructions

❑ Orally recorded instructions

❑ Individual or small group meetings

❑ Student assistants

Other ideas:

❑ _____

❑ _____

How many students may work together in a station?

What are the guidelines for noise levels?

What are students to do when they need supplies or materials?

What combination of options is available when help is needed by students who are working independently and the teacher is directly teaching others?

• Peer collaboration

• Student Assistants

• Task Assistants

• Adult assistance from parent helpers or teaching assistants

• Other ideas:

_____

_____

Kingore, B. (2011). *Tiered Learning Stations in Minutes.* Austin, TX: PA Publishing.

What are students to do with completed products?

What are students to do with works-in-progress that will be continued in the next class period?

What clean up and reorganization responsibilities are required?

What combination of opportunities is provided for students to share ideas and show their work to others?

❑ Sharing time after stations or at the end of the day
❑ Bulletin board or an area in the room where students post their work for others to read and respond
❑ Digital photographs of students at work in stations
❑ Student-written letters to parents about their station-based learning experiences
❑ Student-produced newspaper
❑ Class blog
   Other ideas:

❑ _____

_____

❑ _____

_____

❑ _____

_____

Kingore, B. (2011). *Tiered Learning Stations in Minutes.* Austin, TX: PA Publishing.

# *· 9 ·*
# *Parent Communication*

When parents understand the value of learning stations, they are more likely to appreciate their child's learning experiences at stations. It is beneficial to share information with parents about the objectives and values of stations through letters, school newsletters, parent meetings, or even a workshop for them where they experience station-based learning for themselves.

### Parent Workshop

As parents attend a parent night at school, invite them to complete a worksheet targeting specific skills and then interact in a learning station that applies the same skills with different tasks at varied levels of challenge. Post the skills at the station and ask parents to complete a rubric assessing their learning behaviors and products after they complete the tasks. Follow-up this experience by initiating a discussion with the parents about the similarities and differences between worksheets and station-based learning. Elicit parents' perceptions regarding the mental engagement and transfer potential of the two experiences. Then, provide parents with a copy of The Value of Learning Stations page included in Chapter One. Many parents better understand the value of multi-sensory and diverse-learning-level tasks at stations after this experience. Share additional examples of class rubrics for quality and learning behaviors with parents to help them understand the high expectations specific to students' capabilities and learning objectives.

### Student Letters to Parents

As an authentic writing task, have children write a letter to their parent describing a learning station that they enjoy. Ensure that the students explain how the specific station is important and what they are learning during this time.

### Teacher Letters to Parents

Teachers can also send letters to parents, such as the letter example on the next page that explains the purposes of learning stations. Clarify the depth of learning that is promoted, and invite parental responses and questions.

---

Kingore, B. (2011). *Tiered Learning Stations in Minutes*. Austin, TX: PA Publishing.

## Notes from Parents

Communication is always a two-way street. Encourage parents to share their insights about their child. Invite parents to send notes to school with any questions, observations, or concerns they want to express about station-based learning. It is productive to elicit parents' perceptions of their child's learning and feelings. Some schools report more responses from parents when the teacher sends home note forms to encourage parental communication.

## A Letter to Parents

Dear Families,

Your child participates in tiered learning stations as one important part of learning in our class. Tiered learning stations are classroom work sites where students complete significant learning objectives and flexible group interactions away from their usual table or desk. The learning experiences promote continuous learning for all students at appropriate but different levels of complexity.

Learning stations increase student achievement. They provide a variety of learning experiences that respond to diverse learning strengths and interests to ensure that all children have multiple ways to experience continued learning success. Stations are a significant part of our objective to provide opportunities for children to experience responsibility, decision-making, cooperation, and self-assessment as they engage in learning the crucial skills and concepts in the curriculum.

Your child is able to explain our tiered learning stations to you and is eager to share them with you when you have an opportunity to visit our classroom. Please notice the skills listed at each station to help you understand which learning objectives are incorporated in the learning experiences at that station.

If you have questions or concerns about anything you see or hear, please write or call me so we can discuss them together. Thank you for participating in your child's education.

Sincerely,

Kingore, B. (2011). *Tiered Learning Stations in Minutes*. Austin, TX: PA Publishing.

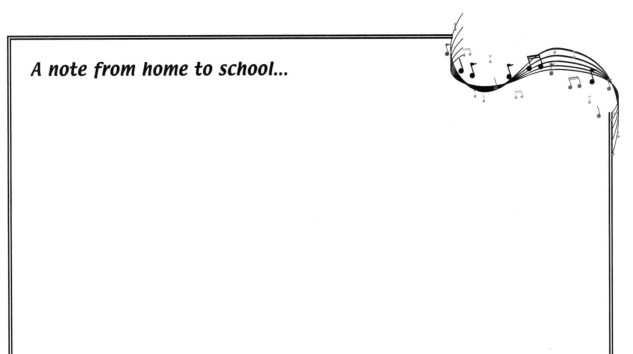

Kingore, B. (2011). *Tiered Learning Stations in Minutes*. Austin, TX: PA Publishing.

Kingore, B. (2011). *Tiered Learning Stations in Minutes*. Austin, TX: PA Publishing.

# *APPLICATION TIME: REFLECT AND SELECT*

# *Jot Down*

### Important Ideas to Share with Parents

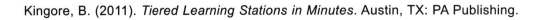

# *10*
# *Common Problems and Possible Solutions*

Save time and frustration by avoiding potential problems that might prevent or limit the application of tiered stations as valuable learning opportunities for students. As a general rule, reason in reverse. Predict potential problems and brainstorm or network with other educators for ways to prevent them. This chapter presents twelve problems that are common to station-based learning environments. Each problem is followed by numerous solutions as possibilities to select from for help.

**1. The time and energy it takes to develop stations**
- Adopt the stations-in-minutes philosophy. Create learning stations that maximize students' achievement and interactive learning while minimizing preparation time. Switch the focus from *beautiful stations* to simple stations with learning opportunities that are *beautiful* because of their educational value and potential for student achievement.
- Simultaneously, save preparation time and increase student ownership by involving students in producing components of stations, such as signs, manipulative, and organizational devices.

**2. Stations that are "fluff" instead of instructionally vibrant; stations that only keep kids busy or entertain them**
- In each station, integrate standards into the learning experience that incorporate the essential outcomes or skills for the grade level. Students deserve to learn at their highest level of readiness and there are numerous concepts and skills they need to learn.
- Refer to the objectives and skills posted at each station and insure that the learning experiences authentically incorporate those standards.

**3. The difficulty of developing tiered tasks at learning stations**
- A teacher must know the curriculum well in order to create tiered learning experiences. When the content is new, work with other teachers to develop tiered variations.
- Elicit student ideas regarding appropriate ways to vary the difficulty and pace of the tasks.
- Initially, use open-ended learning experiences that promote varied degrees of complexity within each student's application of the task.
- Tier graphic organizers by varying the complexity of the graphic and the requirements of the task.
- Begin by tiering one station. When that is working well, initiate tiering at a second station.
- Research the strategy of tiered instruction to refine skills.

**4. A student selects a tiered task that is too difficult**
- Encourage two students to quietly work together on the task. Peer support is an excellent motivational tool and encouragement for struggling students. It also builds the communication

Kingore, B. (2011). *Tiered Learning Stations in Minutes*. Austin, TX: PA Publishing.

skills of both children.
- Post a picture of the task assistant so the students can ask for clarification or help.
- Briefly talk with the student to elicit his or her perceptions and to share your perceptions.
- Contract with the student for the specific tasks to select from when working at a station. Limit the choices to those most applicable to that students' readiness.

5. **A student selects a tiered task that is too easy relative to the student's learning capabilities**
   - Ignore the situation if it happens occasionally. Everyone deserves some time off now and then. For example, even bright adults have been known to watch a television program that is beneath their intellectual level.
   - Communicate with students that any choice is acceptable sometimes, but they learn more when they strive for challenge most times.
   - Intervention is recommended if a student consistently chooses tasks that are too easy. Briefly talk with the student to elicit his or her perceptions and to share your perceptions. Achievement does not increase when students work at a level below their potential. Furthermore, students develop negative habits of mind when no struggle or persistence is required when learning.
   - Contract with the student and specify two or more tasks to select from when working at the station. Limit the choices to those most applicable to that students' readiness and need for challenge.
   - Color code tasks by their complexity level and require students to work at a certain color-coded level. Be sensitive to the danger that this color-coding may be perceived by students and adults as labeling by ability.
   - Require students to write a response about why they chose the task. Leave the prompts open-ended to elicit the student's perception. Briefly meet with the student to discuss the response and motivate appropriate future action.

6. **Adults who do not understand the value of learning stations**
   - Post learning objectives and skills in each station so everyone recognizes the learning connections incorporated into the station tasks.
   - Share information with parents and other adults regarding the educational value of learning stations.
   - Ask students to discuss the value of learning stations and compose a list from their perspectives to post or share with others.

7. **Students playing around at stations instead of working and being productive**
   - Review and assess the learning tasks provided in the station to be certain they represent the intended degree of challenge and interaction.
   - Post a chart of the positive learning behaviors that are expected when the students work independently.
   - Provide a rubric that defines the degrees of quality work on the required learning tasks.
   - Discuss objectives with students before they begin. *What can you do to use this learning time well? What is an important learning goal for you today?*
   - Require students to self-assess and reflect on their accomplishments. A log is a simple tool for organizing this reflection.
   - Allow a smaller number of students in a station.

Kingore, B. (2011). *Tiered Learning Stations in Minutes*. Austin, TX: PA Publishing.

**8. Students hurrying through their regular work to get to stations more quickly**
- Post a rubric clarifying the quality that is expected in regular work and at learning stations.
- Require students to self-assess and reflect upon their accomplishments and what they did to learn. Conduct brief, private discussions with students who do not self-assess accurately.
- Model what quality work looks like, and make it a class expectation that quality work must be completed before proceeding with stations. Students who abuse that requirement lose their privilege of choice.

> *As long as you complete assigned work at an appropriate quality level, you determine when you are ready to go to stations. If you are not completing quality work, you lose the privilege of determining when you go to stations. Then, we must first review your completed work before you move to learning stations.*

**9. Students interrupt when the teacher is directing other students in a small group**
- Discuss with the class your needs as their teacher and the importance of respecting others' right to learn.
- Incorporate a visual signal informing students that you may not be interrupted. Signals that other teachers have successfully used include a tiara, a *Do Not Disturb* sign hung around the neck, and a deserted island graphic in a stand-up picture frame.
- Provide student assistants for tasks and skills.

**10. Stations left in disarray because students do not clean up or reorganize the area**
- Post positive work behaviors.
- Signal a two or three minute warning. That signal prepares students by letting them know the limited time remaining. After the two or three minutes, follow with a transition signal for students to rotate to another station or conclude station time.
- Practice preventative management by pre-planning to avoid messes. For example, place a bucket containing a few inches of water and small sponges beside an art easel. Children simply wipe off the easel each time they paint. (Some students enjoy the water play as much as the painting.)

**11. Students who never get to learning stations because their other work is not finished quickly enough**
- Avoid only using stations as alternatives for students who finish early.
- Incorporate a rotation system. As long as students are responsible and working, they move into stations when it is their time.
- Evaluate independent work. Ensure that it is the appropriate tier of challenge for each student. Students who are frustrated or overwhelmed need intervention and task accommodation.

**12. Students who finish the learning tasks at a station before it is time to change stations**
- Provide one extra station: *Extra! Extra! Learn All About It!* Children who complete quality work at an assigned station can go to the extra station containing a potpourri of thinking, art, or problem-solving activities that can quickly be added to or changed.
- Use an open-choice planning board that allows students to change stations when they complete tasks rather than on a timed schedule.

Kingore, B. (2011). *Tiered Learning Stations in Minutes.* Austin, TX: PA Publishing.

## APPLICATION TIME: REFLECT AND SELECT

# But what about...?

**Potential Problems**

**Possible Solutions**

**Unknowns**

Kingore, B. (2011). *Tiered Learning Stations in Minutes*. Austin, TX: PA Publishing.

# The Tool Box

The Tool Box is a set of simple and effective graphics, organizers, and templates that expedite the implementation of tiered learning stations. To facilitate applications, this chapter overviews each of the tools on the CD. Small illustrations of each tool accompany the brief explanations in this overview.

The *Tool Box CD* included with this book contains full-sized versions of each tool to download for clear and convenient printing. The text of each tool on the CD is customizable. Before duplicating tools for student use, adapt any tool to respond to the specific content and objectives that are relevant to current topics of study. In addition to teacher applications, students can directly use the CD to complete an application of a tool on their computers.

Some tools on the CD, such as the station icons, are provided in different sizes, in colors, and in black and white to accommodate a range of instructional applications. Software programs on many computers allow further adaptations to change the color and size of the tools.

## TIERED LEARNING STATION PLAN TEMPLATES

Full-sized versions of these six templates used in the tiered learning station plans in Chapter 4 are included on the CD and can be customized.

**Design-an-Academic-Game**

**Editing Bookmarks**

**Error Analysis**

**Grocery Budget Sheet**

**I Want to Read about...**

**Math Error Analysis**

Kingore, B. (2011). *Tiered Learning Stations in Minutes.* Austin, TX: PA Publishing.

## CHECKLISTS

Checklists are used by teachers and students to assess how well particular segments of learning are working. They have the potential to succinctly document learning and focus on important standards. The caution, however, is to avoid checklists composed of such an infinite list of isolated skills that the marking process is laborious and consumes excessive instructional time. Use brief lists to guide assessment and provide a system to effectively document progress and achievement.

Whether instructing a small group or the entire class, teachers can use a checklist to organize a quick notation of students' continued skill progress and learning needs over time. Teachers also provide students with a checklist of skills to guide their monitoring of their own competencies in a skill area. A self-assessment checklist that reviews procedures and sequences enables students to successfully complete more complex learning processes, such as revising their written work. A checklist effectively scaffolds such learning experiences for students experiencing difficulty.

**Checklist Jot Down**

On this checklist, list the names of the students in a small group. Then, jot down observed skill applications or reteaching needs while directing instruction or when observing students interacting at learning stations. If preferred, add dates to note when a student attains proficiency.

### Checklist Jot Down

Jot down observations and insights. Check *proficient* when applicable.

| Students: | Skill: | Skill: | Skill: |
|---|---|---|---|
| | ❑ PROFICIENT | ❑ PROFICIENT | ❑ PROFICIENT |
| | ❑ PROFICIENT | ❑ PROFICIENT | ❑ PROFICIENT |
| | ❑ PROFICIENT | ❑ PROFICIENT | ❑ PROFICIENT |
| | ❑ PROFICIENT | ❑ PROFICIENT | ❑ PROFICIENT |
| | ❑ PROFICIENT | ❑ PROFICIENT | ❑ PROFICIENT |
| | ❑ PROFICIENT | ❑ PROFICIENT | ❑ PROFICIENT |

Kingore, B. (2011). *Tiered Learning Stations in Minutes.* Austin, TX: PA Publishing.

Kingore, B. (2011). *Tiered Learning Stations in Minutes.* Austin, TX: PA Publishing.

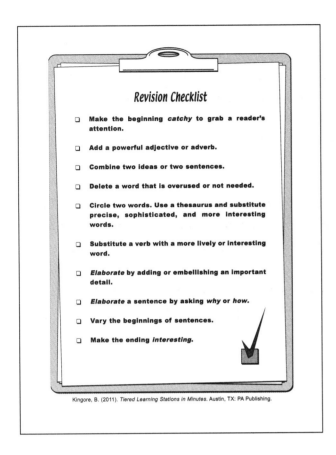

## Revision Checklist

A checklist guides students' self-assessment and enables them to take responsibility for continued achievement with more complex processes. Adapt this checklist to scaffold students' sequencing of revision.

# CONTRACTS

Contracts provide a means for teachers to ensure that students have differentiated learning experiences while encouraging students to plan, goal set, and engage in record keeping to expedite their achievement. Additionally, contracts are an effective management tool for students who would benefit from challenge or replacement tasks beyond the core curriculum. Contracts enable students to choose the sequence in which they complete stations and manage the length of time they spend at each station.

To empower students as active participants in their learning, students are encouraged to review their work, assess its strengths, and determine potential areas or skills for growth and development. Students and teachers collaboratively set goals to accomplish those changes and establish contracts that focus students on what work is necessary to enable their growth and development. Some learning experiences and skills might be part of every student's contract while others are particular to a specific student or group. Contracts for learning stations generally include:

* Learning tasks for students;
* Directions for appropriate and productive learning behaviors;
* As much choice as appropriate to the learner;
* A timeline for completing work; and
* Directions for assessment and what to do when work is complete.

### Primary Learning Station Contract

Offer more structure and support to students with entry-level independent skills. Write the required stations, learning tasks, and designated time frame on a contract before meeting with the student. During the brief meeting, present additional stations and tasks from which the student can select to foster continuous learning. Whenever feasible, ensure that students retain some choice of station tasks to increase their motivation to excel and their ownership in the process.

---

**Learning Station Contract**

BEGINNING DATE _____        ENDING DATE _____

*I selected these learning tasks:*        I WILL WORK:
☐  During the learning station time.
Station: _____        ☐  When I compact out of _____
Task: _____        _____.

ASSESSMENT:
Station: _____        ☐  A checker will review each task as I
Task: _____        finish. If correct, that
contract task is stamped.
If not, I rework
Station: _____        the task until it is
Task: _____        correct.

☐  I will self-assess daily in my station log.
☐  I will exceed expectations by _____
_____        *My teacher selected these*
_____        *learning tasks:*

**MY TEACHER WILL CHECK MY WORK:**        Station: _____
☐  As I finish each activity.        Tasks: _____
☐  Once a week.        and _____
☐  During our conference on _____        Station: _____
Task: _____
STUDENT _____        or _____
DATE _____        Station: _____
Task: _____
TEACHER _____        or _____
DATE _____

Kingore, B. (2011). *Tiered Learning Stations in Minutes*. Austin, TX: PA Publishing.

### Learning Station Contract

Self-motivated students with independent skills can take the lead when contracting which work to complete during station time. Meet briefly with a student to initiate the contract. Specify the required learning stations and tasks for the student to list on the contract, negotiate a time frame of several days or a few weeks for completion, and designate the number of additional stations and tasks the student needs to select and complete. Students paste station icons on the contract and add the name of the learning task at each station. Finally, discuss the student's specialization and facilitate those decisions.

---

**Learning Station Contract**

DATE INITIATED _____        DATE DUE _____        DATE COMPLETED _____
Based upon my assessed learning needs, these stations and tasks are required.

I have selected these _____ additional stations and tasks to complete.

**Specialization.** I want to spend more time at the _____ station.
My learning target:

I will use these resources:

My finished product will be:

**Teacher–Student Time**
✓  When your name is called, you meet with me to reflect and assess.
✓  Be prepared to explain how you met and how you exceeded expectations.
✓  Select one item to represent the results of your effort, continuous learning, and management.
✓  I will randomly select a second piece to review from your station log and folder.
✓  We will discuss your self assessments of your learning behaviors and products, and collaboratively determine your contract grade.

STUDENT _____        DATE _____
TEACHER _____        DATE _____

Kingore, B. (2011). *Tiered Learning Stations in Minutes*. Austin, TX: PA Publishing.

Kingore, B. (2011). *Tiered Learning Stations in Minutes*. Austin, TX: PA Publishing.

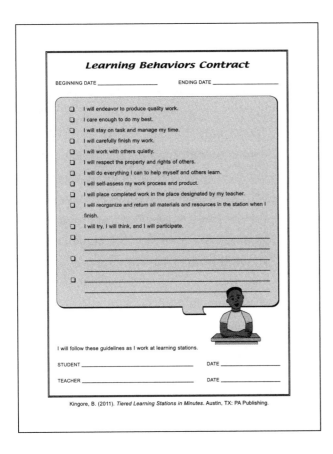

Kingore, B. (2011). *Tiered Learning Stations in Minutes*. Austin, TX: PA Publishing.

## Learning Behaviors Contract

Students use this contract to commit to the learning behaviors they will practice and demonstrate during station-based learning. Learning behavior contracts clarify expectations to students, and students can better hit a target that is clear.

# LEARNING BEHAVIOR RUBRIC

A learning behavior rubric is an assessment tool that communicates relevant high expectations for learning. Students use the rubric to self-assess their effort and accomplishments as they complete learning tasks. The objective is to communicate to students the behaviors they should practice to promote learning, demonstrate responsibility, and develop independent learning skills.

Work with the students to determine and prioritize a list of the behaviors students demonstrate when they are actively engaged in learning. In response to students' ages and backgrounds, the teacher's role in the process modulates from more directive to a facilitator following the leads of students. Guide students in a discussion of the parameters that are relevant to each learning behavior when students work independently, in groups, or at learning stations. This collaborative experience of clarifying behaviors and establishing a continuum of the levels of positive learning behaviors can result in fewer classroom management problems and increased student task-commitment and production. Students feel more ownership when they participate in the process of establishing classroom expectations.

- Clarify which behaviors are nonnegotiable. For example, it is not debatable *if* clean up will occur, only *how* it will be completed.

Kingore, B. (2011). *Tiered Learning Stations in Minutes*. Austin, TX: PA Publishing.

- State the behaviors in positive terms as much as possible, communicating what *to do* rather than what *not to do*.
- Less may be best. Keep the list as brief as is appropriate.
- Consider creating a contract specifying these behaviors for students to sign, such as the Learning Behavior Contract shared previously.

Organize the results of this discussion into a learning behavior rubric to succinctly communicate behavior decisions. The three examples of learning behavior rubrics shared here range from simple to more complex. Scan these examples to prompt thinking and decisions regarding the behavior levels to target on a particular learning behavior rubric. Letter grades or percents can be substituted for the evaluative words used as headings. Once established, post these behaviors in the classroom, share them with parents, and have students keep a copy in their work folders for continued reference.

> **Students who share ownership in establishing classroom expectations are more likely to be responsible, productive learners.**

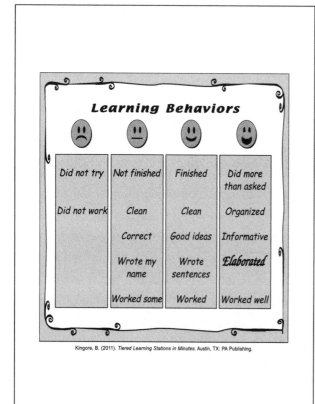

Kingore, B. (2011). *Tiered Learning Stations in Minutes*. Austin, TX: PA Publishing.

### Learning Behavior Rubric Tier I

This rubric is appropriate for learners with beginning-level reading skills. It is also effective for English language learners. When they complete learning tasks, children self-assess by referring to the rubric and drawing on their work the face they earned.

Kingore, B. (2011). *Tiered Learning Stations in Minutes*. Austin, TX: PA Publishing.

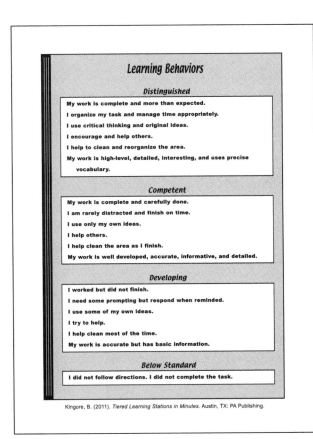

### Learning Behaviors

#### Distinguished

My work is complete and more than expected.

I organize my task and manage time appropriately.

I use critical thinking and original ideas.

I encourage and help others.

I help to clean and reorganize the area.

My work is high-level, detailed, interesting, and uses precise vocabulary.

#### Competent

My work is complete and carefully done.

I am rarely distracted and finish on time.

I use only my own ideas.

I help others.

I help clean the area as I finish.

My work is well developed, accurate, informative, and detailed.

#### Developing

I worked but did not finish.

I need some prompting but respond when reminded.

I use some of my own ideas.

I try to help.

I help clean most of the time.

My work is accurate but has basic information.

#### Below Standard

I did not follow directions. I did not complete the task.

Kingore, B. (2011). *Tiered Learning Stations in Minutes*. Austin, TX: PA Publishing.

## Learning Behavior Rubric Tier II

This rubric elaborates words and ideas to clarify the specific variations of quality while communicating learning behavior expectations to students. When students complete learning tasks, they self-assess by referring to the rubric and recording which level they earned by their work. If preferred, students can circle each statement to document the highest level they achieve for each criterion.

### Learning Behaviors

NAME _____ DATE _____

| Below expectations | Developing learner | Practitioner | Autonomous citizen |
|---|---|---|---|
| Less effort than expected | On task but needs some urging | Uses time appropriately with minimal supervision | Self-motivated without adult supervision |
| Disrespectful | Usually respectful but interrupts others | Respects and helps others; shares | Respectful; encourages and redirects others |
| Unable to explain applications | Applies skills but inconsistent | Accurately applies skills | Clearly explains applications and transfers skills |
| Gives up easily | Works to improve when encouraged | Works to achieve and seeks help when needed | Works to continuously improve; accepts challenges |
| Lacks correct content | Accurate but basic content without elaboration | Well developed content; beyond basic facts; appropriate vocabulary | In-depth content; well supported; precise vocabulary |
| Does not assess or reflect without prodding | Generally self-assesses and reflects without prodding | Appropriate response and good analysis in self-assessment and reflection | Critical thinker; high-level reflection and interpretation |

I met expectations by:

What I did to exceed expectations:

Kingore, B. (2011). *Tiered Learning Stations in Minutes*. Austin, TX: PA Publishing.

## Learning Behavior Rubric Tier III

This rubric further elaborates learning behaviors. It is a more specific tool that mature students can use daily to evaluate their productive work behaviors and establish their goals for continuous improvement. When students complete learning tasks, they self-assess by referring to the rubric and recording which level they earned by their work. If preferred, students can circle each statement to document the highest level they achieve for each criterion.

Kingore, B. (2011). *Tiered Learning Stations in Minutes*. Austin, TX: PA Publishing.

# *LEARNING STANDARDS POSTERS*

A learning standards poster is a communication tool for students and adults. The laminated poster lists the essential concepts and skills that are the learning targets in a grade-level content area. Each week, place a check beside the skills incorporated into the content of the station for that week. The poster helps to specify to students the focus of station-based learning and to document to observers that standards are embedded in the content of each station.

As a simple means to develop a poster of learning standards for every station, review district learning standards to determine which are particularly applicable for each station. Educators may also elect to refer to the Common Core State Standards (2010) to guide their decisions regarding the most relevant standards to include.

List key words of the year-long content area standards on a simple graphic and laminate that paper. As a visual reference, post the applicable list at students' eye-level in each station. Check the standards that currently apply to the learning tasks at each station, and then wipe those checks off and check different standards as the focus changes. Scan these examples from different grade level content areas to prompt specific applications of learning standards posters.

**Reading Learning Standards**

**Math Learning Standards**

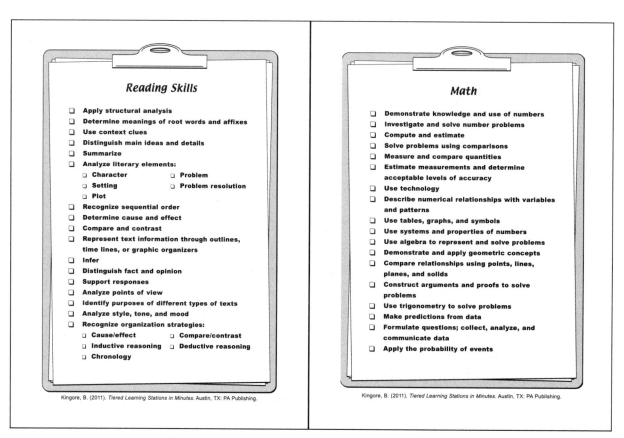

*Reading Skills*

- ❑ Apply structural analysis
- ❑ Determine meanings of root words and affixes
- ❑ Use context clues
- ❑ Distinguish main ideas and details
- ❑ Summarize
- ❑ Analyze literary elements:
  - ❑ Character    ❑ Problem
  - ❑ Setting    ❑ Problem resolution
  - ❑ Plot
- ❑ Recognize sequential order
- ❑ Determine cause and effect
- ❑ Compare and contrast
- ❑ Represent text information through outlines, time lines, or graphic organizers
- ❑ Infer
- ❑ Distinguish fact and opinion
- ❑ Support responses
- ❑ Analyze points of view
- ❑ Identify purposes of different types of texts
- ❑ Analyze style, tone, and mood
- ❑ Recognize organization strategies:
  - ❑ Cause/effect    ❑ Compare/contrast
  - ❑ Inductive reasoning    ❑ Deductive reasoning
  - ❑ Chronology

Kingore, B. (2011). *Tiered Learning Stations in Minutes.* Austin, TX: PA Publishing.

*Math*

- ❑ Demonstrate knowledge and use of numbers
- ❑ Investigate and solve number problems
- ❑ Compute and estimate
- ❑ Solve problems using comparisons
- ❑ Measure and compare quantities
- ❑ Estimate measurements and determine acceptable levels of accuracy
- ❑ Use technology
- ❑ Describe numerical relationships with variables and patterns
- ❑ Use tables, graphs, and symbols
- ❑ Use systems and properties of numbers
- ❑ Use algebra to represent and solve problems
- ❑ Demonstrate and apply geometric concepts
- ❑ Compare relationships using points, lines, planes, and solids
- ❑ Construct arguments and proofs to solve problems
- ❑ Use trigonometry to solve problems
- ❑ Make predictions from data
- ❑ Formulate questions; collect, analyze, and communicate data
- ❑ Apply the probability of events

Kingore, B. (2011). *Tiered Learning Stations in Minutes.* Austin, TX: PA Publishing.

Kingore, B. (2011). *Tiered Learning Stations in Minutes.* Austin, TX: PA Publishing.

**Primary Science Learning Standards**          **History/Social Studies Learning Standards**

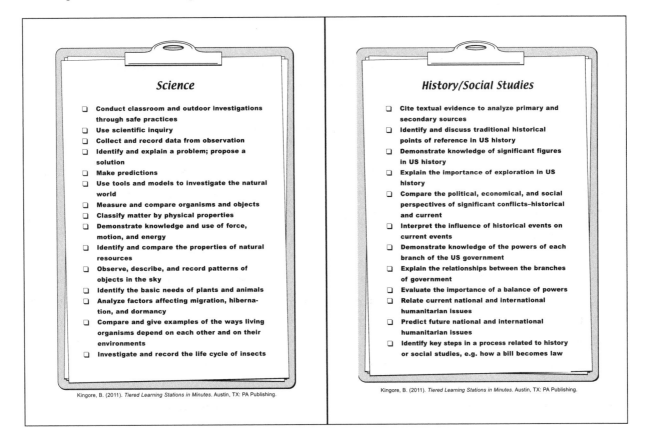

*Science*

❏ Conduct classroom and outdoor investigations through safe practices
❏ Use scientific inquiry
❏ Collect and record data from observation
❏ Identify and explain a problem; propose a solution
❏ Make predictions
❏ Use tools and models to investigate the natural world
❏ Measure and compare organisms and objects
❏ Classify matter by physical properties
❏ Demonstrate knowledge and use of force, motion, and energy
❏ Identify and compare the properties of natural resources
❏ Observe, describe, and record patterns of objects in the sky
❏ Identify the basic needs of plants and animals
❏ Analyze factors affecting migration, hiberna-tion, and dormancy
❏ Compare and give examples of the ways living organisms depend on each other and on their environments
❏ Investigate and record the life cycle of insects

Kingore, B. (2011). *Tiered Learning Stations in Minutes.* Austin, TX: PA Publishing.

*History/Social Studies*

❏ Cite textual evidence to analyze primary and secondary sources
❏ Identify and discuss traditional historical points of reference in US history
❏ Demonstrate knowledge of significant figures in US history
❏ Explain the importance of exploration in US history
❏ Compare the political, economical, and social perspectives of significant conflicts–historical and current
❏ Interpret the influence of historical events on current events
❏ Demonstrate knowledge of the powers of each branch of the US government
❏ Explain the relationships between the branches of government
❏ Evaluate the importance of a balance of powers
❏ Relate current national and international humanitarian issues
❏ Predict future national and international humanitarian issues
❏ Identify key steps in a process related to history or social studies, e.g. how a bill becomes law

Kingore, B. (2011). *Tiered Learning Stations in Minutes.* Austin, TX: PA Publishing.

# STATION LOGS

As a part of their continued development of responsibility and analytical thinking skills, require students to maintain records of their station activities that document what they learn through each experience. With modeling and guided practice, students can learn to manage the paper work that supports stations as viable learning opportunities. Provide appropriate variations of reflective tech-niques and templates to enable students of all ages to successfully maintain records of their work.

Station logs are a reflective device. In stations logs, students maintain a running record of the tasks they engage in and then self-assess the quality of their learning behaviors and resulting products. These logs enable students and teachers to easily track what has been accomplished and which stations need to be completed next. Each log should contain a copy of the learning behavior rubric for student reference. A station log can be a small spiral notebook or a student-made booklet, such as the station log templates shared here, in which students date and record learning responses. To use a station log template, students cut out and staple together a cover, a learning behavior rubric, and multiple copies of the response page. On each response page, students write what task they completed at a station, explain how they used the skill(s) checked on the learning standards poster, and self-assess the grade or level they earned according to their demonstrated learning behaviors during the process of completing station tasks.

Kingore, B. (2011). *Tiered Learning Stations in Minutes.* Austin, TX: PA Publishing.

Kingore, B. (2011). *Tiered Learning Stations in Minutes.* Austin, TX: PA Publishing.

## Station Log Booklet for Young Children

This log requires less writing for young students or special-needs students who simply cut out and paste the icon picture of the station they worked in and draw the face they earned for their quality of effort and learning behaviors. Children then write words or a sentence to note which learning task they completed and what they think about the experience. When appropriate, increase the use of self-assessment prompts to encourage students to elaborate their perspectives about their work.

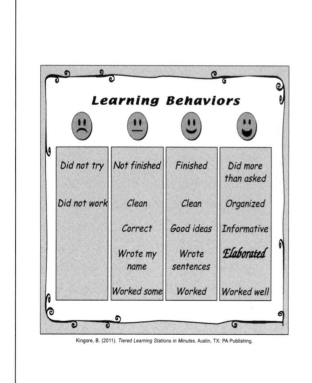

Kingore, B. (2011). *Tiered Learning Stations in Minutes.* Austin, TX: PA Publishing.

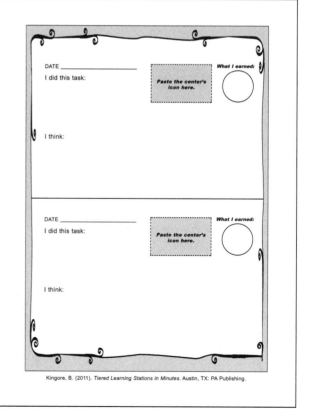

Kingore, B. (2011). *Tiered Learning Stations in Minutes.* Austin, TX: PA Publishing.

Kingore, B. (2011). *Tiered Learning Stations in Minutes.* Austin, TX: PA Publishing.

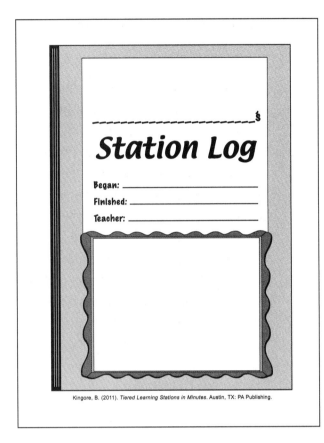

Kingore, B. (2011). *Tiered Learning Stations in Minutes*. Austin, TX: PA Publishing.

### Station Log Booklet for Older Learners

This log requires students to write a brief summary of which tasks they did in the station, which skills they applied, and what they learned. Students are expected to refer to the skills posted in the station and explain how they applied those specific skills. They also use the learning behavior rubric to assess what they earned by their effort and work. The station log is completed every day or each day that stations are used. The illustration frame on the bottom of the cover fosters visual-spatial connections. Students complete the illustration of their choice or draw designated responses, such as:

*Draw a favorite place.*
*Draw a favorite thing to do.*

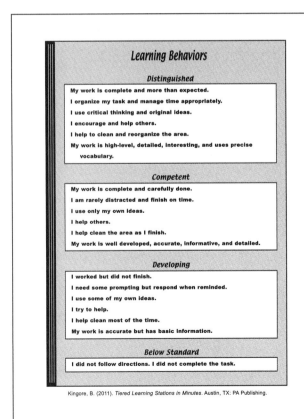

Kingore, B. (2011). *Tiered Learning Stations in Minutes*. Austin, TX: PA Publishing.

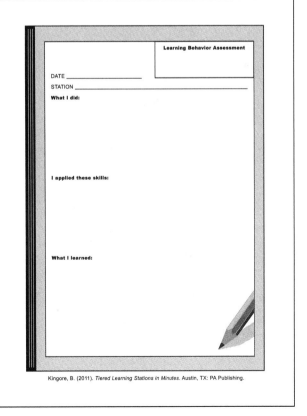

Kingore, B. (2011). *Tiered Learning Stations in Minutes*. Austin, TX: PA Publishing.

Kingore, B. (2011). *Tiered Learning Stations in Minutes*. Austin, TX: PA Publishing.

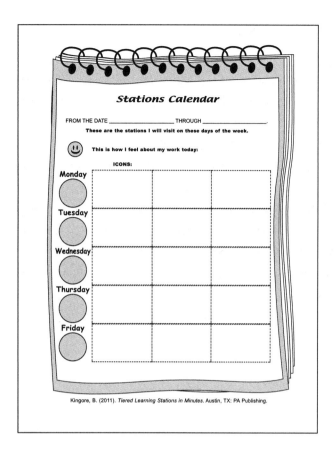

### Station Calendar

As an initial training device for students with less-developed independent work skills, use a weekly Station Calendar. Each day, students cut out and glue the icon(s) for the station(s) they complete. There is a space by each day for multiple icons or one icon plus a student-written sentence about the work. In the circle, they record the grade or face they earned by their effort and demonstrated learning behaviors.

Daily or weekly, the class meets to debrief. They discuss what went well and how to improve the learning experience. In pairs or trios, students share the results of their work as adults circulate and assess by jotting down observations.

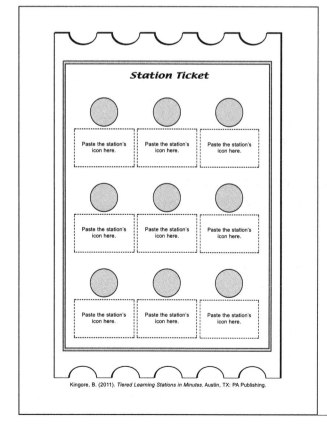

### Station Ticket

This record keeping format is particularly applicable for young and special-needs students because it requires limited writing. After completing a station, students paste the corresponding icon onto the ticket. They self-assess by drawing in the circle the face or grade they earned for their effort, learning behaviors, and work. Initially, this ticket allows children to complete stations in the designated rotation order. As independent skills increase, the ticket allows students to complete every station in the sequence of their choice before they can repeat working in a station.

# STUDENT REFLECTION

Reflection or metacognition is related to students' ability to analyze their thinking strategies and learning process to transfer knowledge from one situation to another. Baker and Brown note that it involves two basic components:

1. Students' awareness of the processes they need to successfully complete a task, and
2. Students' cognitive monitoring–the ability to determine if the task is being completed correctly and initiate corrections as appropriate (1984).

Students' reflections express their perceptions of their process and achievements. As they complete a learning task at a station, students reflect upon and write about what they did and what they learned. These reflections guide students' awareness of how their effort results in achievement and in what ways they are changing as learners. This technique activates process engagement and is valuable as a formative assessment to guide lesson adaptations.

---

**Self-assessment prompts**

- *This is how I feel about my work today.*
- *This reminds me of...*
- *One thing I did well...*
- *One thing I intend to work more on...*
- *Something that really surprised me is...*
- *The part that caused me the most trouble is...*
- *I had to really think about it, but I figured out...*
- *I will remember...*
- *Something similar to this is...*
- *I can use this information to...*
- *I have an idea! I can use the skills of _____ to teach someone how to...*

**Maintain student interest in recording learning responses**

- *Use different prompts to increase students' mental engagement.*
- *Vary the length of prompts to elicit shorter or more elaborate responses.*
- *Change the format. Use the 3-2-1 exit ticket for a fresh visual appeal.*
- *Incorporate choice. As an alternative process, provide all students with a copy of a numbered list of eight or more reflective sentence stems. Every day, either assign prompts by telling students which numbers to respond to, or invite students to select one or more prompts they want to use for reflection in their logs.*
- *Elicit students' ideas for sentence stem prompts and reflection tools.*

---

The applications in this section intend to guide students' reflective thinking. While blank paper can be used, templates in the form of picture prompts, sentence stems, a 3-2-1, a Time to Reflect, and a Consider All Angles are visually appealing as they scaffold students' thinking and help them succinctly organize their responses. The emphasis is on analytical thinking rather than the length of the response.

Kingore, B. (2011). *Tiered Learning Stations in Minutes*. Austin, TX: PA Publishing.

## Picture reflection prompts

These picture reflection prompts are intended for young or special needs children because the prompts only require entry-level reading and writing skills. The intent of these prompts is to begin to foster the routine of self assessment.

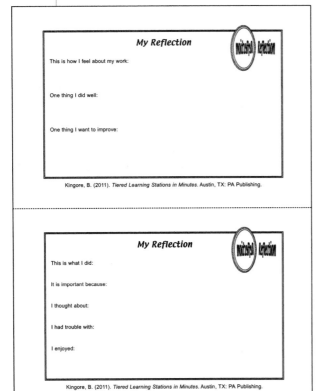

## My Reflection

Vary these simple sentence stems to focus students' reflections. As appropriate to their age and readiness, students can respond with pictures, symbols, words, or sentences.

Kingore, B. (2011). *Tiered Learning Stations in Minutes.* Austin, TX: PA Publishing.

---

**Learning Station Task**

The learning task I completed was _____
_____.

✓ I chose this task because it was:
- ☐ Easy            ☐ Challenging        ☐ Quick to complete
- ☐ Interesting     ☐ Fun

✓ I wanted to:
- ☐ Work with a friend    ☐ Work by myself    ☐ Help someone
- ☐ Finish quickly        ☐ Work with someone for help

I think _____
_____
_____

Kingore, B. (2011). *Tiered Learning Stations in Minutes*. Austin, TX: PA Publishing.

---

**Learning Station Task**

The learning task I completed was _____
_____.

✓ I chose this task because it was:
- ☐ Easy            ☐ Challenging        ☐ Quick to complete
- ☐ Interesting     ☐ Fun

✓ I wanted to:
- ☐ Work with a friend    ☐ Work by myself    ☐ Help someone
- ☐ Finish quickly        ☐ Work with someone for help

I think _____
_____
_____

Kingore, B. (2011). *Tiered Learning Stations in Minutes*. Austin, TX: PA Publishing.

## Learning Station Task

This reflective tool is particularly useful when it appears that a student is selecting learning tasks that are too simple to foster continuous learning. When appropriate, require students to write a response reflecting why they chose a particular learning station task. Leave the prompts open-ended to elicit the student's perception. Briefly meet with the student to discuss the response and motivate appropriate future action.

---

**3** Things I did:
_____

**2** Things I want to learn:
_____

**1** Thing I would like to change:
_____

Kingore, B. (2011). *Tiered Learning Stations in Minutes*. Austin, TX: PA Publishing.

---

**3** Skills I used:
_____

**2** Strengths in my work:
_____

**1** Connection I made:
_____

Kingore, B. (2011). *Tiered Learning Stations in Minutes*. Austin, TX: PA Publishing.

## 3-2-1

Students write brief responses to the 3-2-1 prompts and add quick sketches or symbols to illustrate their response. This exit ticket tool is a popular variation as it requires minimum handwriting while still emphasizing thinking.

---

Kingore, B. (2011). *Tiered Learning Stations in Minutes*. Austin, TX: PA Publishing.

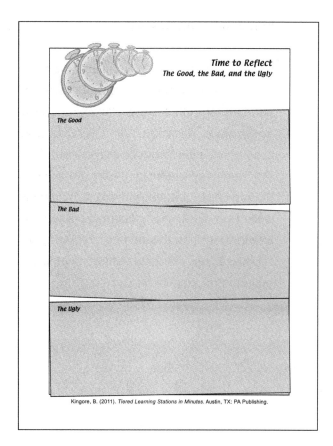

## Time to Reflect: The Good, the Bad, and the Ugly

This tool invites students to reflect upon the positive as well as the more negative aspects of a topic or event. It is particularly applicable as a device to foster students' responses to the issues and ethical connections of a topic.

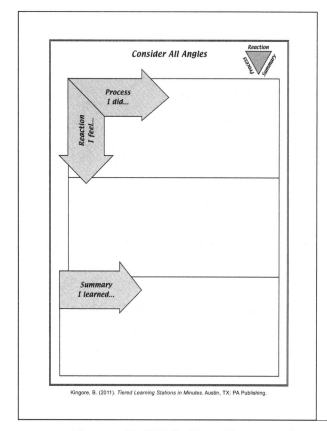

## Consider All Angles

Consider All Angles emphasizes process engagement, social-emotional connections, and summarization. Process engagement and emotional connections promote students' mental engagement and self assessment. Summarization is an effective strategy to promote memory.

Kingore, B. (2011). *Tiered Learning Stations in Minutes*. Austin, TX: PA Publishing.

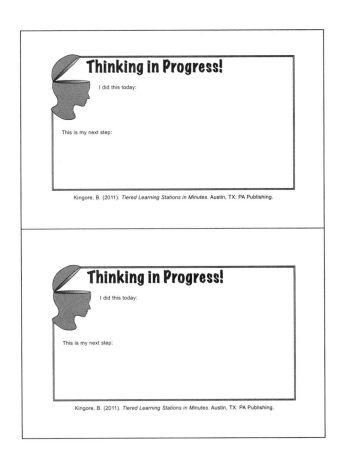

Kingore, B. (2011). *Tiered Learning Stations in Minutes.* Austin, TX: PA Publishing.

Kingore, B. (2011). *Tiered Learning Stations in Minutes.* Austin, TX: PA Publishing.

### Thinking In Progress

Some students may not successfully complete a learning task at a station in a single visit because of difficulties they experience or because they are embellishing and developing their product with depth. Provide copies of a *Thinking In Progress* form that students complete and post with their work as a status note. The sample provided here is a template for a Thinking In Progress form that helps students goal set and plan their continued work.

# VISUAL LEARNING TOOLS

The CD includes learning station icons, alphabet figures, numeral figures, and polygon figures as visually-appealing figures to use throughout classroom stations. The station icons are effective when used as a communication device to represent each learning station. Use different sizes of the icons in color or black and white to increase application possibilities.

* Post a large copy of each station icon to mark the location of that station and help students associate the icon with the station.
* Use small copies of the station icons to organize planning boards or rotation posters used for student placement at stations.
* Provide small copies that students cut out as needed to complete their station logs, tickets, or calenders when they finish working a learning station.

The alphabet figures, numeral figures, and polygon figures provide whimsical appeal to concepts and skills particularly in math and language arts. These simple graphics are useful year-round as decorative accents that add visual appeal and continuity to classroom displays, bulletin boards, and stations.

## Station Icons

## Alphabet Figures : Upper Case and Lower Case

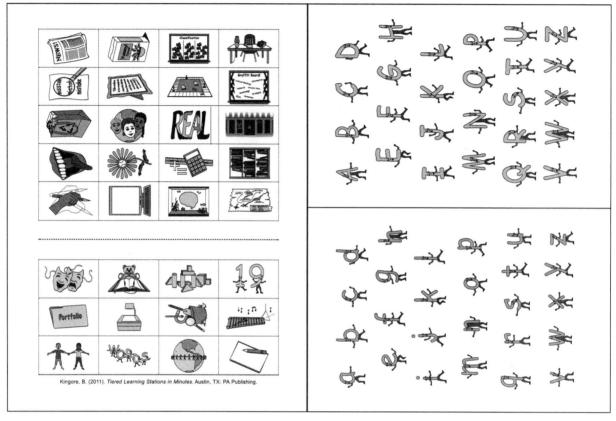

Kingore, B. (2011). *Tiered Learning Stations in Minutes*. Austin, TX: PA Publishing.

## Numeral Figures

## Polygon Figures

Kingore, B. (2011). *Tiered Learning Stations in Minutes*. Austin, TX: PA Publishing.

# *References*

Association for Supervision and Curriculum Development. (2006). *Building academic vocabulary: Research-based, comprehensive strategies. Research Report.* Alexandria, VA: Author.

Baker, L. & Brown, A.L. (1984). Metacognitive skills and reading. In P. David Pearson (Ed.), *Handbook of reading research.* New York: Longman.

Barretta, G.(2007). *Dear deer: A book of homophones.* New York: Henry Holt.

Berk, L. & Winsler, Z. (1995). *Scaffolding children's learning: Vygotsky and early childhood education.* Washington, DC: National Association for the Education of Young Children.

Caine, R., Caine, G., Klimek, K., & McClintic, C. (2004). *12 Brain/mind learning principles in action.* Thousand Oaks, CA: SAGE Publications.

Council of Chief School Officers and the National Governors Association. (2010). *Common core state standards for English language arts and literacy in history, social studies, and science.* Washington, D.C., Author.

Crews, D. (1986). *Ten black dots.* NY: Greenwillow Books.

Dweck, C. (2007). *Mindset: New psychology of success.* New York: Ballantine Publishing.

*Education Week.* (2009). Oral-language practice helps English-language learners. *29* (8), 8.

Edwards, P. (1996). *Some smug slug.* New York: HarperCollins.

Gifford, M. & Gore, S. (2008). *The effects of focused academic vocabulary instruction on underperforming math students.* Research Report. Alexandria, VA: Association for Supervision and Curriculum Development.

Hattie, J. & Timperley, H. (2007). The power of feedback. *Review of Educational Research, 77,* 81-112.

Kingore, B. (2011). *Tiered Learning Stations in Minutes.* Austin, TX: PA Publishing.

Illingworth, M. (1996). *Real-life math problem solving.* NY: Scholastic.

Kingore, B. (2007). *Assessment: Timesaving procedures for busy teachers* (4th ed.). Austin, TX: Professional Associates Publishing.

Kingore, B. (2008). *Developing portfolios for authentic assessment, PreK-3.* Thousand Oaks, CA: Corwin Press.

Kingore, B. (2009). *Recognizing gifted potential: Professional development presentation.* Austin, TX: Professional Associates Publishing.

Krashen, S. (1993). *The power of reading: Insights from the research.* Englewood, CO: Libraries Unlimited.

Lester, H. (1997). *Author: A true story.* Boston: Houghton Mifflin.

Marzano, R. (2004). *Building background knowledge for academic achievement: Research on what works in schools.* Alexandria, VA: Association for Supervision and Curriculum Development.

Marzano, R. (2006). *Classroom assessment & grading that work.* Alexandria, VA: Association for Supervision and Curriculum Development.

Marzano, R. (2010). Meeting students where they are: Using games to enhance student achievement. *Educational Leadership 67*(5), 71-72.

McGrath, B. (2000). *Skittles Riddles.* Watertown, MA: Charlesbridge.

McTighe, J. & O'Connor, K. (2005). *Seven practices for effective learning.* Educational Leadership, 63 (3), 10-17.

Mensa. (1996). *Genius.* San Francisco: Chronicle Books.

Mensa. (1996). *Genius for kids.* San Francisco: Chronicle Books.

National Association for the Education of Young Children & National Association of Early Childhood Specialists in State Departments of Education. (2003). *Early childhood curriculum, assessment, and program evaluation: Building an effective, accountable system in programs for children birth through age 8. Position statement.* Washington, DC: Author.

National Reading Panel (NRP). (2000). *Teaching children to read: An evidence-based assessment of the scientific research literature on reading and its implications for reading instruction.* Jessup, MD: National Institute for Literacy.

Neuschwander, C. (2003). *Sir Cumference and the sword in the cone.* Watertown, MA: Charlesbridge.

Payne, R. (2003). *A framework for understanding poverty* (3rd ed.). Highlands, TX: Aha! Process.

Reynolds, P. (2003). *The Dot.* Cambridge, MA: Candlewick Press.

Schotter, R. (2006). *The Boy who loved words.* New York: Schwartz & Wade Books.

Schwartz, D. (1999). *If you hopped like a frog.* NY Scholastic.

Scieszka, J. (1995). *Math curse.* New York: Penguin Putnam.

Shepard, L. (1997). *Measuring achievement: What does it mean to test for robust understanding?* Princeton, NJ: Educational Testing Service.

Slocumb, P. (2008). Giftedness in poverty. In M. Gosfield (Ed.), *Expert approaches to support gifted learner.* Minneapolis, MN: Free Spirit Publishing.

Sousa, D. (2006). *How the brain learns* (3rd ed.). Thousand Oaks, CA: Corwin Press.

Steinberg, L. (2003). *Thesaurus rex.* Cambridge, MA: Barefoot Books.

Steiner J. (1998). *Look alikes.* NY: Little, Brown.

Steiner J. (1999). *Look alikes jr.* NY: Little, Brown.

Stiggins, R. (2007). *Student-involved assessment for learning* (5th ed.). Upper Saddle River, NJ: Prentice Hall.

Stronge, J. (2002). *Qualities of effective teachers.* Alexandria, VA: Association for Supervision and Curriculum Development.

Sullo, B. (2009). *The Motivated student: Unlocking the enthusiasm for learning.* Alexandria, VA: Association for Supervision and Curriculum Development.

Sylwester, R. (2003). *A biological brain in a cultural classroom* (2nd ed.). Thousand Oaks, CA: Corwin Press.

Tang, G. (2002). *The Best of times.* NY: Scholastic.

Tedrow, M. (2008). Best practices: The Miracle of choices. *Teacher Magazine.* teachermagazine.org/tm/articles/2008/05/28/35tin_ted

Viorst, J. (1978). Alexander who used to be rich last Sunday. NY: Atheneum.

Vygotsky, L. (1962). *Thought and language.* Cambridge: MIT Press.

Wiggins, G. & McTighe, J. (2005). *Under-standing by design (*2nd ed.). Alexandria, VA: Association for Supervision and Curriculum Development.

Willis, J. (2006). *Research-based strategies to ignite student learning: Insights from a neurologist and classroom teacher.* Alexandria, VA: Association for Supervision and Curriculum Development.

Willis, J. (2007a). *Brain-friendly strategies for the inclusion classroom.* Alexandria, VA: Association for Supervision and Curriculum Development.

Willis, J. (2007b). The neuroscience of joyful education. *Engaging the Whole Child,* 64, Summer.

Winebrenner, S. & Brulles, D. (2008). *Cluster grouping handbook: How to challenge gifted students and improve achievement for all.* Minneapolis, MN: Free Spirit Publishing.

Wolfe, P. (2001). *Brain matters: Translating research into classroom practice.* Alexandria, VA: Association for Supervision and Curriculum Development.

Wormeli, R. (2006). *Fair isn't always equal: Assessing and grading in the differentiated classroom.* Portland, ME: Stenhouse Publishers.

Zaccaro, E. (2007). *25 real life math investigations that will astound teachers and students.* Bellevue, IA: Hickory Grove Press.